Praise for *The Son of David*

"*The Son of David* is a book about Jesus. Nancy takes the reader through the plot-line of redemption revealed in the historical narratives. All of the heroic figures in the Old Testament were mere pointers to the greater Savior, Redeemer, Shepherd, and King who was to come, namely, Jesus. This book argues very convincingly that all the wonderful promises presented in shadow form have found their ultimate completion in the one who reigns perfectly over his kingdom. Thank you, Nancy, for your humble heart and prayer that desire to see more and more people give their affections to this amazing paradoxical kingliness that leads us to serve others with humility and courage."

Kathleen Um, Director of Family and Women's Ministries, Citylife Presbyterian Church, Boston, Massachusetts

"As Christian growth leaders, we are constantly searching for Bible study material that is scripturally sound and grounded on biblical truths. Nancy Guthrie has a wonderful gift of keeping her studies interesting and challenging. *The Son of David*, perhaps her most inspiring work in the Seeing Jesus in the Old Testament series thus far, is no exception. No matter where students are in their spiritual walk or in their realm of biblical knowledge, they will be inspired as they discover Jesus in the books of the Old Testament."

Kitty Kosman, Christ the King Lutheran Church, Memphis, Tennessee

"Nancy Guthrie's Seeing Jesus in the Old Testament series brings a depth to women's ministries that we desperately need. When you complete *The Son of David*, you will have a wonderful grasp of the historical books, but also your heart will melt as you see Jesus unveiled in every book. John Piper has said, 'Beholding is becoming,' and this is the kind of study that helps us behold our God and, in so doing, become the godly women we long to be."

Dee Brestin, author, *Idol Lies* and *The God of All Comfort*

Praise for the Seeing Jesus in the Old Testament Series:

"I am thankful for a series that ties together the truths of all of Scripture, from beginning to end. Nancy's humble and genuine examples, careful study, and thoughtful application questions have encouraged women at our church to know and love Jesus, even as they come to know and understand the Old Testament. 'By grace alone' is evident throughout this study."

Melissa Kummerer, Director of Community Life, All Saints Presbyterian Church, Austin, Texas

"These studies are a rare blend of being theologically rich but very down-to-earth, personable, and practical. I am confident when I pick up a study guide by Nancy that it is well researched, challenging to either a young or mature believer, and consistently Word-centered and gospel-centered."

Yvonne Shorb, Calvary Bible Fellowship Church, Coopersburg, Pennsylvania

"Our women's groups have delighted in this Bible study treasure. Many women were introduced for the first time to the Old Testament and were able to dig in, understand, and savor its rich meaning. Each week I've loved hearing the ah-hahs of those in my group as the Scripture revealing Christ opens up and begins to anchor their faith more deeply."

Becky Moltumyr, Director of Women's Ministry and LIFEgroup Connection, Brookside Church, Omaha, Nebraska

"I am constantly searching for authors who can further equip me to teach Christ from all of Scripture. Nancy Guthrie's Seeing Jesus in the Old Testament series helps readers connect the New Testament to the Old Testament and shows how both point to Christ. Her thought-provoking and practical study questions have helped me turn lectures into discussions. This series has been transformative for me, my staff, and my students. I highly recommend it."

Rev. David Dobbs, Pastor of Student Ministries, First Presbyterian Church, Rome, Georgia

The Son of David

The Son of David

*Seeing Jesus in
the Historical Books*

(A 10-Week Study)

nancy guthrie

CROSSWAY®

WHEATON, ILLINOIS

Trade paperback ISBN: 978-1-4335-3656-4
PDF ISBN: 978-1-4335-3657-1
Mobipocket ISBN: 978-1-4335-3658-8
ePub ISBN: 978-1-4335-3659-5

Library of Congress Cataloging-in-Publication Data

Guthrie, Nancy.
　　Son of David : see Jesus in the historical books (a 10-week study) / Nancy Guthrie.
　　　　pages cm.—(Seeing Jesus in the Old Testament ; Book 3)
　　Includes bibliographical references.
　　ISBN 978-1-4335-3656-4
　　1. Bible. O.T.—Study and teaching. 2. Jesus Christ—Biblical teaching—Study and teaching. I. Title.
BS1193.G88　　　　2013
222'.0071—dc23　　　　　　　　　　　　　　2013000956

Crossway is a publishing ministry of Good News Publishers.

VP		30	29	28	27	26	25	24	23	22	21
21	20	19	18	17	16	15	14	13	12	11	10

To the son of David in our family, Matt Guthrie.
May Jesus be to you . . .
the greater Joshua who leads you into rest,
the greater Savior who makes you right in God's eyes,
the greater Redeemer who secures your inheritance,
the greater Shepherd who restores your soul,
the greater King who rules over your will,
the greater Wisdom who shows you what to do,
the greater Mediator who was willing
to perish so you won't have to.

Contents

Before We Get Started

A Note from Nancy

When Jesus began his ministry, he began with the words, "The time is fulfilled, and the kingdom of God is at hand" (Mark 1:15). Those in his day who heard him say these words had a leg up on most of us in understanding what he meant. They had a sense of kings and kingdoms that we don't have, living in our modern era. But if we really want to understand the person of Jesus and respond rightly to him, we have to understand what it means that he is a king. And if we want to rightly understand the purpose of Jesus's ministry, we have to understand what it means that he taught his disciples to pray for his kingdom to come. And the best way to understand the kingdom and the king is to begin in the historical books of the Old Testament, which create for us a context in which we can better understand the kingdom of God as it once was, as it is now, and as it will one day be.

There are three essential parts to this study. The first is the personal time you will spend reading your Bible, seeking to strengthen your grip on its truths as you work your way through the questions provided in the Personal Bible Study section of each week's lesson. This will be the easiest part to skip, but nothing is more important than reading and studying God's Word, expecting that he will meet you as you do. Because we will cover large chunks of Scripture that I will not have time to read through and explain in the Teaching Chapters or videos, the foundational understanding you gain through your time doing the Personal Bible Study will be essential.

As you work on the Personal Bible Study, try not to become frustrated if you can't come up with an answer to every question or if you're not sure what the question is getting at. The goal of the questions is not necessarily to record all of the "right" answers, but to get you into the passage and thinking it through in a fresh way. Certainly some answers to your lingering questions will become clearer as you read the chapter or watch the video and as you discuss the passage with your group.

The second part of each lesson is the Teaching Chapter, in which I seek to explain and apply the passage we are studying. If your group is using the accompanying video series, the Teaching Chapter in the book is the same content I present on the videos. If you are using the videos, you can go ahead and read the chapter as a preview, if you'd like, or simply sit back and watch the video. Or you may prefer to come back and read the chapter *after* watching the video to seal in what you've heard. It's up to you. You can also download an audio or video version of the Teaching Chapters at http://www.crossway.com.

At the end of each Teaching Chapter is a short piece called "Looking Forward," which will turn your attention to how what we've just studied in that particular historical book offers insight into what is still to come when Christ returns. In these books of the Bible we find not only the history of what God has done in the past to establish his kingdom but also insight into what he is doing now and is yet to do in the future when "the kingdom of the world has become the kingdom of our Lord and of his Christ, and he shall reign forever and ever" (Rev. 11:15). This part of the Teaching Chapter is not included in the video, so if you are in a group using the video to take in the teaching, be sure to go back to this part of the Teaching Chapter each week after watching the video, as part of your group discussion or on your own.

The third part of each week's lesson is the time you spend with your group sharing your lives together and discussing what you've learned and what you're still trying to understand and apply. A discussion guide is included at the end of each week's lesson. You may want to follow it exactly, working through each question as written. Or you may just want to use the guide as an idea starter for your discussion, choosing the questions that suit your group and discussing key insights you gained through the Personal Bible Study and Teaching Chapter.

Each aspect is important—laying the foundation, building on it, and sealing it in. We all have different learning styles, so one aspect of the study will likely have more impact on you than another, but all three together will help you to truly "own" the truths in this study so that they can become a part of you as you seek to know your covenant God in deeper ways.

I've put together the sections of this study in a way that offers flexibility in how you can use it and in how you can schedule your time working through it. If you are going to use it for a ten-week book study, you will want to read the Teaching Chapter in Week 1, "The Kingdom of God," before the first meeting. (There is no Personal Bible Study section for the first week.) From then on, participants will need to come to the group time having completed the Personal Bible Study section of the next week's lesson, as well as having read the Teaching Chapter. You may want to put a star beside questions in the Personal Bible Study and underline key passages in the chapter that you want to be sure to bring up in the discussion. During your time together each week, you will use the Discussion Guide to talk through the big ideas of the week's lesson.

There is a great deal of material here, and you may want to take your time with it, letting its foundational truths sink in. To work your way through the study over twenty weeks, break each week into two parts, spending one week on the Personal Bible Study section—either doing it on your own and discussing your answers when you meet, or actually working through the questions together as a group. Over the following week, group members can read the chapter on their own and then come together to discuss the big ideas of the lesson.

If you are leading a group study, we would like to provide you with a leader's guide that has been developed specifically for this study. To download the free leader's guide, go to http://www.SeeingJesusinthe OldTestament.com.

My prayer for you, as you begin this study of the kingdom of God in the historical books, is that it will help you to have a better handle on the story line of the Old Testament. I grew up being taught the many Bible stories of the Old Testament. And I am so grateful for it! But only recently would I have been able to verbalize the most basic flow of Israel's history from their emergence from slavery in Egypt to the time of Christ. My understanding of where and when certain aspects of Israel's history—like the time of the judges, the northern and southern king-doms, and the two different exiles and returns—was just a fuzzy mess in my mind. Maybe you can relate. Or maybe you are newer to the Bible and you really have little sense of Israel's history or why it would even matter to know about it. Wherever you are in terms of your grasp of the historical story line and timeline of the people of God in the Old Testament, I hope this study will take you a step further. I pray that this study will cause you to see the greatness of King Jesus in new and awe-inspiring ways that will enable you to worship him more fully. I pray it will compel you to want to bend your will and bow your knee before him in greater submission to his kingdom authority in your life.

—Nancy Guthrie

Week 1

The Kingdom
of God

Teaching Chapter

Your Kingdom Come

I smiled at a recent tweet sent by our friend Gabe deGarmeaux. It was a picture of his wife and daughter preparing to board their flight to Orlando, and it said, "Watch out Disney, I'm on my way with two more princesses."

Now, I did not grow up immersed in as much Disney-princess culture as today's children. In my day *The Magical World of Disney*, the only way you could see Disney movies outside of the theater, aired on Sunday nights at 6:00. And of course, we were always heading out to Sunday night church when it came on. Heaven to me at that point in my life was a Sunday night when, for some reason, we got to stay home from church and indulge ourselves in Disney magic.

But everything has changed since my childhood. First came VHS and then DVD and now digital downloads. Today, even in the car, on our way to school or soccer practice, we can inundate our sons and daughters with handsome princes and beautiful princesses. And what do our daughters want to be on dress-up day? Disney princesses, of course. In fact, I've noticed that some little girls insist on wearing their princess gowns and tiaras pretty much every day of the year.

And, really, who wouldn't want to be a princess with perfect hair, an 18-inch waist, a closet full of ball gowns, and living in a kingdom with a handsome prince and a cadre of servants? I think we can all agree we'd be up for that. But most of us, at one point or another, realize all of our wishing upon a star has proven to have no power to make it so.

Perhaps the reason that stories of kings and kingdoms capture our interest is that they reflect the childlike longings we've trained ourselves to deny. Perhaps there is something deep inside us that knows there really is a kingdom in which we could be cherished by the prince and protected by the king—a kingdom in which no one has to be afraid or go hungry but everyone enjoys peace and safety and perfect love.

Friends, this is not just the fodder of fairy tales or simply escapist denial. It is the hope the Bible holds out to us. The story of the Bible is really the story of a kingdom that you and I are invited to enter into and experience in part now and in fullness forever. It's the story of the true king who rules over his people with perfect love and justice.

The Kingdom as It Once Was

The story of the true king and his kingdom begins this way:

> In the beginning, God created the heavens and the earth. (Gen. 1:1)

> *The Kingdom of God throughout the Bible and throughout history is always this: "God's people in God's place under God's rule."*
> —Graeme Goldsworthy

The Bible begins by telling us that God is the majestic king over the world. His kingdom is the heaven and the earth he created from nothing. Adam and Eve lived in the perfect garden paradise called Eden as the Creator-King's loyal subjects, enjoying his provision and his presence right there with them. Here is the kingdom of God as it once was: *God's people*, Adam and Eve, living in *God's place,* the garden of Eden, under *God's rule*, his clear instruction to be fruitful, increase in number, fill the earth, and subdue it, and to eat freely of every tree in the garden except for one. In fact, the kingdom of God throughout the Bible and throughout history is always this: "God's people in God's place under God's rule."[1]

God's people, Adam and Eve, lived in God's place, the garden of Eden, and everything about it was good—perfectly good—until they

[1]Graeme Goldsworthy, *Gospel and Kingdom*, in *The Goldsworthy Trilogy: Gospel and Kingdom, Gospel and Wisdom, The Gospel in Revelation* (Exeter: Paternoster, 2000), 54.

rebelled against God's rule. A rival kingdom invaded God's kingdom in the form of a serpent who tempted Adam and Eve to reject God as their king. He told them they could be kings in their own kingdom, that their king was withholding something good from them. But it was a lie. And when Adam and Eve rebelled against the loving rule of their king, everything that was once so beautiful became broken. They were forced out of God's kingdom of Eden because, you see, no one who refuses to live in obedience to the King has a place in his kingdom.

But God, the good king, was not content to make peace with this ongoing alienation. So he began working out his plan to restore his people to his kingdom. He did this by declaring war—not on those who had rebelled against him but against sin and death. And ever since then, two opposing forces have been at war in the world: the kingdom of God and the kingdom of Satan, the seed of the woman and the seed of the Serpent. The Bible makes clear that God is accomplishing this restoration of his kingdom, not through an instantaneous edict but through a lengthy historical process. God began working out his plan to bring his people back to his place to live under his rule by calling one man, Abraham, to himself, making incredible, undeserved promises to him. God promised Abraham that he would be the father of a great people and that he would give this people a place, the land of Canaan, where they would live under his loving rule. When this family grew and was enslaved outside of the place God intended for them, he brought them out and gave them his law so that they would know how to live under his rule in his land. This was to be a land flowing with milk and honey, reminiscent of the garden paradise God's people had once enjoyed. And if they obeyed him there, they would live there enjoying its abundance forever.

This is the part of God's story we're going to focus in on in this study. The kingdom established in the Promised Land of Canaan has much to reveal to us in shadow form about the larger kingdom that God is bringing and the greater king who sits on its throne.

⁓ In Joshua, as we witness Moses's successor lead the people of God into rest in the land that God gave to them, we'll see how the greater Joshua, Jesus, leads his people into rest.

~ In Judges we'll see how God used a series of flawed deliverers to save his people when they cried out to him, all of whom point to a more perfect deliverer who was yet to come. We'll see that Jesus saves people who are bent on doing what is right in their own eyes and transforms us into people who are right in God's eyes.

~ In the book of Ruth we'll meet Boaz, who shows, in shadow form, how our kinsman-redeemer, Jesus, will cover us with his protection, fill us with his provision, and pay the required cost to secure our stake in God's kingdom land.

~ In 1 Samuel we'll witness a boy from Bethlehem, David, go out alone against the great enemy who taunts God's people with threats of enslavement, Goliath. With one smooth stone, David will crush Goliath's head. And we will see that he foreshadows another boy born in Bethlehem who will go out alone against the great enemy of sin and death who taunts God's people with threats of eternal enslavement. We'll see that on the cross, and by his resurrection from the dead, Jesus crushed the head of our great enemy.

~ In 2 Samuel we'll look at David, the king God set on the earthly throne over his people. We'll see in him shadows of his greater son who is even now seated on David's royal throne in heaven and will one day descend to reign in the New Jerusalem forever and ever.

~ In 1 Kings we'll take a tour of the golden era of Israel during King Solomon's reign—when everything was as it should be and the whole world marveled at Israel's abundance and the wisdom of her king. We'll see glimpses of the way the kingdom of God will one day be when we have peace on every side and the whole world streams to the throne of our king to give him tribute.

~ In 2 Kings we'll trace the kings who sat on David's throne after him, most of whom had no heart for God as David had. It will become clear that a greater king was needed—a king who would rule in righteousness, not rebellion; a king who would be faithful, not idolatrous; a king who would love God's Word rather than ignore it. In stark contrast to all of the kings who sat on Israel's throne, we'll see the King of kings and Lord of lords who sits on David's throne, before whom the whole world will one day bow.

⟩ In Ezra, who taught the Scriptures to God's people, we'll see shadows of the one who was the fulfillment of all that the Scriptures teach. In Nehemiah, who rebuilt the walls of Jerusalem using ruined stones, we'll see shadows of the one who is building his church with living stones—the lives of those who have been reclaimed from the rubble of sin.

⟩ And finally, in Esther, we'll see echoes of the one who, not at the risk of his life but at the cost of his life, interceded to accomplish the deliverance of God's people.

As we work our way through this history of Israel, we'll witness the people of God repeatedly proving to be rebellious to God's rule and ultimately being exiled from the place that God had given to them. Remember: no one who refuses to live in obedience to the King has a place in his kingdom. Still, God's commitment remained to have a people for himself, living in his place under his loving rule. In exile, a faithful remnant hung onto God's promise sent through his prophets that he would not only bring the people back but would also come and reign as their king. Through his prophet Isaiah, God told them what the coming king's government would be like:

> Of the increase of his government and of peace
>   there will be no end,
> on the throne of David and over his kingdom,
>   to establish it and to uphold it
> with justice and with righteousness
>   from this time forth and forevermore. (Isa. 9:7)

The prophet Micah told them where this king would come from:

> But you, O Bethlehem Ephrathah,
> who are too little to be among the clans of Judah,
> from you shall come forth for me
>   one who is to be ruler in Israel,
> whose coming forth is from of old,
>   from ancient days. (Mic. 5:2)

And the prophet Zechariah spoke of his entrance into his royal city:

> Rejoice greatly, O daughter of Zion!
>   Shout aloud, O daughter of Jerusalem!

Behold, your king is coming to you;
    righteous and having salvation is he,
humble and mounted on a donkey,
    on a colt, the foal of a donkey. (Zech. 9:9)

When the faithful remnant of God's people was able to return to the land, they waited there for the greater king and the greater kingdom to come.

The Kingdom at Hand

And then the King came, saying:

The time is fulfilled, and the kingdom of God is at hand; repent and believe in the gospel. (Mark 1:14–15)

> *All that the kingdom of Israel had been pointing toward for centuries was becoming a reality with the coming of the true King.*

When Jesus became flesh and dwelt among us, the kingdom of heaven broke into the realm of earth. Have you ever been outside while it is raining and yet you can see the sun breaking through the clouds somewhere in the sky? That is a picture of this reality. The incarnation of Christ was the glory of heaven breaking through the veil that separates heaven and earth. All that the kingdom of Israel had been pointing toward for centuries was becoming a reality with the coming of the true King.

Yet Jesus didn't really seem like a king, at least not like the kind of king the Israelites were expecting. Kings are born in palaces, not in cattle stalls. Kings expect to be served, not to serve. Kings robe themselves in royal garments, not with a towel so that they can wash everyone's feet. Kings are crowned with gold, not with thorns.

Clearly Jesus was not going to be a king, and his was not going to be a kingdom like the kings and kingdoms they were used to. This became evident when Jesus stood up and began to teach. The paradoxical wisdom of the kingdom of God he spoke of was quite different from the accepted wisdom in the kingdoms of the world. He said that the greatest people in God's kingdom are those who serve. He said that we should love our enemies and that it is more blessed to give than to receive. He said that the only way to save your life is to lose it.

Jesus taught people to pray, "Our Father in heaven, hallowed be your name. Your kingdom come, your will be done, on earth as it is in heaven" (Matt. 6:9–10). How do you think his will is done in heaven? In his heavenly throne room all creatures serve him with a glad yes, yes, yes. There is no pause to determine whether his command suits their preferences or will fit in their busy schedules. Of course, this is not at all what it's like here on earth. Jesus taught us to pray that this disparity of obedience between heaven and earth will be eradicated. And one day it will be.

Throughout his earthly ministry Jesus was constantly pulling back the curtain to reveal what the kingdom of God will be like when his kingdom comes in all of its glorious fullness. He healed those with diseases, showing that sickness and disease have no place in his kingdom. He commanded the demons to depart, because nothing evil will have its way forever in his kingdom. He stilled the sea, showing that all nature submits to his command in his kingdom. He fed multitudes, revealing the abundant satisfaction to be found in his kingdom. He raised Lazarus to life, previewing the day when the bodies of all his kingdom subjects will be raised to resurrection life.

In the obedience of his life, Jesus revealed the perfect righteousness that permeates his kingdom. By his sin-atoning death, Jesus proved that sin and death no longer get the last word in his kingdom. In his resurrection he previewed the future hope of those who will populate his kingdom. And in his ascension he entered into the current realm of his kingdom.

Jesus came telling us exactly how we should respond to his kingdom at hand. He did not say, "Follow my example; try real hard to live like me." Instead, he said, "Repent and believe in the gospel." What does that mean? To repent is much more than shedding tears over your past. It is to identify your sin and sinfulness and turn your back on it so that you can pursue Christ. It is to turn away from greed and toward gospel-empowered generosity. It is to turn from always giving in to lust without a thought and toward battling against it through the power of the Holy Spirit. It is to turn from your determination to run your own life the way you please to saying "Jesus is Lord" and to really mean it. That's repentance.

To believe is, first, to know the content of the gospel, that anyone can be right with God—acquitted, forgiven, restored, adopted—through trusting faith in Jesus's atoning death and victorious resurrection. But to believe is more than just knowing this. It is to come under it, to rest in it, to take it into the very center of your life.

Jesus comes to us as our true King, saying to each of us: "Repent and believe the gospel." So I have to ask you, as we get started in this study, *have you ever come to repentance?* Life in the kingdom is not about self-improvement, trying to become a better person or a more spiritual person. To be in the kingdom of God is to recognize that your sin is an offense to the king and to choose to abandon it so that you might pursue and please the king. *Have you believed—going beyond just knowledge about Christ to putting your whole confidence in him?* If you walk away from this study having learned everything there is to know about the history books of the Old Testament, yet you never turn toward the King in repentance and belief, all the time you spent increasing your knowledge will serve only to make you even more responsible for your defiant rebellion or your informed apathy toward the King.

The Kingdom as It Is Now

While the kingdom was "at hand" at the King's first coming, it did not come in power but rather in weakness. On Pentecost God poured out his Spirit on his people, empowering his people to take the gospel of his kingdom to the ends of the earth. Today, the kingdom of God is spreading across the world as the gospel goes out and is embraced by those who repent and believe.

The kingdom of God is no longer bound up with one nation in one country. That was a picture of things to come. God's kingdom comes now as people bow to Jesus as king. At its simplest, the kingdom is where the King is; it's where he rules and reigns. As he rules and reigns in your life, that is the kingdom. As he rules and reigns amongst his people, the church, that is the kingdom. Everywhere his will is done—everywhere his justice is accomplished, his righteousness is lived out, his gospel is loved—is the kingdom. Everywhere his subjects are saved by his hand, everywhere his enemies are vanquished by his power, everywhere his commandments are obeyed, that is the kingdom.

So if you want to know how to enter the kingdom of God, it is to pray, "Your kingdom come, your will be done in my life, in my heart, on this earth, in the same way that your will is gladly done by all of the angels of heaven." It is to say, "Jesus is Lord"—Lord over my choices, Lord over my finances, Lord over my future—Jesus is Lord over this family, Lord over this church, Lord over this company, Lord over this land. To become a Christian is to ask God to set up his throne as the supreme King of our hearts. We don't receive Christ as Savior and then at some later point, as it suits us, make him Lord. Jesus is Lord. And when he opens our blind eyes to see ourselves as dead in our sin and makes us alive, we are awakened to the reality of his supreme lordship. Calling upon Christ for salvation is bowing the knee to his kingship. It is never anything less than that, because he is never anything less than the true King. What saves people is the grace of the King who reigns over them.

So if being a citizen of the kingdom of God is welcoming the rule and reign of Christ, it makes no sense that someone who has truly come under the loving rule of King Jesus would continue to live a life of pursuing ongoing rebellion against the ways of the King and the kingdom. But we must also admit that we all have territory in our lives, in our hearts, that we have yet to cede to the rule of our King, areas about which we say to our King: "Everything else in my life you can have your way with, but not this. This, I will continue to manage and control."

Oh, how we need our good King to refuse to surrender his claim to any and every area of our lives! How we need his kingdom to come to us in all of its loving rule!

And it does come to us even now as we live in this world as citizens of heaven. For now, the kingdom of God is *God's people* (all of those joined to Christ, living on earth as citizens of heaven) in *God's place* (the temple being built with living stones, the church) *under God's rule* (the blessings of the new covenant). For now, the kingdom of God is a community of sinners washed clean by the blood of the King, seeking to please the King, longing for the return of the King.

And evidently it is not only redeemed people who long for the return of the King. All of creation longs for the kingdom to come in all its fullness and glory.

> For the creation waits with eager longing for the revealing of the sons of God. For the creation was subjected to futility, not willingly, but because of him who subjected it, in hope that the creation itself will be set free from its bondage to corruption and obtain the freedom of the glory of the children of God. (Rom. 8:19–21)

All of creation is crying out in longing for the King to come, for the kingdom to come. That's because, while the kingdom of God is here now, it is not here in the way it will be one day. For now, we live in an in-between time—in between the time Jesus established his kingdom and the time when he takes his throne and exercises his authority over all things. For now, every skirmish with that same old sin, every bout of cancer, every corrupt politician, every report of abuse, every picture of a hungry child, and every breakup of another family just increases our longing for our King to come and set things right for good. We want our King to come in justice, punishing evil and rewarding good. We want his reign of grace and truth to spread throughout the world, throughout the entire creation.

And one day it will. One day his kingdom will come. His will *will* be done on this earth in the same way it is done in heaven. Heaven will come to earth when Jesus, the King of heaven, comes to earth.

The Kingdom as It Will Be

When Jesus comes again, God's kingdom will be completely restored— even better than it once was in Eden—in what the Bible calls the new heaven and the new earth. God's people, people from every tribe, tongue, and nation, will live in God's place, the new heaven and the new earth, under God's rule, where we will worship him around his throne.

Do you sometimes wonder what God is doing in the world, where this world is headed? The goal of God's work in history is this: his kingdom come, his will done on earth as it is in heaven. When his kingdom comes in all its fullness, all will acknowledge his lordship. At the name of Jesus every knee will bow, in heaven and on earth and under the earth, and every tongue will confess that Jesus Christ is Lord, to the glory of God the Father (Phil. 2:10–11). What is God's by right will be his in fact. God's people, all of those whose names are written in the Book of Life, will be in God's place, which will extend to every corner of the earth, under the rule of the King of kings.

No more rebellion will be tolerated when his kingdom comes. "That ancient serpent, who is called the devil and Satan, the deceiver of the whole world" (Rev. 12:9), will be destroyed forever by King Jesus so that a loud voice in heaven will be heard saying, "Now the salvation and the power and the kingdom of our God and the authority of his Christ have come, for the accuser of our brothers has been thrown down, who accuses them day and night before our God" (Rev. 12:10).

No more sickness will be tolerated when his kingdom comes. No more mental illness, no more birth defects, no more metastasized cancer, no more diabetes, no more drug addiction.

No injustice will be perpetrated when his kingdom comes. No ethnic cleansing, no economic oppression, no sexual abuse.

No sinful patterns will be accommodated when his kingdom comes. No gossipy comments. No envious thoughts. No lustful looks.

No natural disasters will bring catastrophe when his kingdom comes. No one will drown in a tsunami or starve in a famine.

When his kingdom comes there will be no darkness, only glorious light; no more tears, only ongoing joy; no more death, only never-ending life.

Your kingdom come, Lord Jesus!

My friend Gabe sent another tweet a couple of days after he had sent the tweet warning Disney that he was on his way with two more princesses. It was a picture of the crowd walking down Main Street at Disneyworld. It said, "Looking forward to the day I get to be in a real kingdom with the King." Me too, Gabe. Because while it will be wonderful to live in a kingdom where there is no more sickness, no more pain, and no more tears, the best thing about the kingdom will be the

King seated on the throne at the very center. The face that will capture our attention will be the face of the King. This is why it makes no sense for those who want nothing to do with Jesus to say they want to go to heaven and have every right to go to heaven. It is the presence of Jesus, the King, that makes heaven what it is now and what it will be when his kingdom comes to earth. And his kingdom *is* going to come; *he* is going to come.

> Behold, I am coming soon. . . . I, Jesus, have sent my angel to testify to you about these things for the churches. I am the root and the descendant of David, the bright morning star. (Rev. 22:12, 16)

The Son of David is going to come and reign. Throughout this study of the Old Testament historical books, we'll have the opportunity to see more clearly the kind of king who is coming to reign over us forever.

There is only one kingdom that proves true, one kingdom that will last forever, one kingdom with a King on the throne worthy of worship and able to reign over this world and to reign in our hearts in true righteousness. And it is not wishing upon a star that will make this dream come true. It is bowing before this great King and gladly coming under his righteous rule. His reign in your life begins with the prayer he taught us to pray: "Our Father in heaven, hallowed be your name. Your kingdom come."

Discussion Guide

Your Kingdom Come

Getting the Discussion Going

1. Throughout history and in literature and the movies there are plenty of kings and kingdoms. What are some of the good things and some of the bad things we've picked up from world history, great literature, and modern films about how kings and kingdoms work?

Getting to the Heart of It

2. Perhaps you've never thought of the garden of Eden as a kingdom. What can we learn about how our King interacts with and what he expects from his kingdom subjects from what we know about the experience of Adam and Eve in the garden of Eden?

3. Nancy went through a list of what we'll get to observe in this study and how we'll see Jesus in the Old Testament historical books, Joshua through Esther. What did you hear that was new or intriguing to you, or perhaps different from how you've studied these books in the past?

4. The Gospel writers tell us that Jesus began his ministry by proclaiming that the kingdom of God was "at hand." If Jesus said the kingdom was "at hand," why did he teach his disciples to pray for the kingdom to come?

5. When Jesus announced that the kingdom was at hand, he called people to "repent and believe in the gospel." What does it mean to repent? And what does it mean to "believe in the gospel?"

6. How does participating in a Bible study about the historical books, in which we're seeking to discover how they point us toward Christ, honor our King?

Getting Personal

7. In regard to our submission to the King, one approach is to listen to his Word and then evaluate whether we agree with it before we choose to obey. Another approach is to say yes even before we know what it is because we are confident his commands are always for our good. What difference do you think it would make in your life if you were to have a "yes" posture to God's Word rather than a posture of "wait and see"?

Getting How It Fits into the Big Picture

8. Several times we heard Graeme Goldsworthy's formula for the kingdom of God: God's *people* in God's *place* under God's *rule*, though these things look slightly different in different eras or ages of the kingdom. See if together you can identify who God's people were in creation, then in Old Testament history, and then who they are in our current age and in the age to come. Try to do the same thing for God's place and God's rule.

Joshua

Personal Bible Study

Joshua

The Bible is all about God's promise of an inheritance in the kingdom of God. The book of Joshua is the story of how Joshua led the people of Israel to take possession of their inheritance in the earthly kingdom of God, Canaan. And as we study the book of Joshua in light of the New Testament, this book helps us understand how our greater Joshua, Jesus, leads us to take possession of all we stand to inherit in the heavenly kingdom of God, the new heaven and the new earth. Since we are spending only one week on this book, we won't be able to take in all of its rich detail, but we will seek to grasp how it fits in God's story of the outworking of his plan to redeem all things through Christ. (Because we are covering the entire book in one week, there are quite a few questions, but your answers do not need to be lengthy. In most cases, they can be a phrase or a sentence or two.)

Entering the Land

1. Before starting Joshua, go back to Deuteronomy 34:4. On what basis are the Israelites intending to inhabit the land of Canaan? Or, what has led them to this place of camping on the east side of the Jordon River?

2. Perhaps it bothers you a bit that it appears that God is going to give land that seemingly belongs to the Canaanite tribes to the people of Israel. But who does the land really belong to, according to Psalm 24:1 and Leviticus 25:23?

3. Read Joshua 1:1–9, noting what God promises and what God commands.

God's promise to Joshua:

    v. 2

    v. 5

    v. 9

God's command to Joshua:

    v. 6

    v. 7

    v. 8

    v. 9

4. Read Joshua 2:1–14. What does Rahab, a prostitute among pagans, know about the land, the Israelites, and God, and what does she want?

5. Read Joshua 2:24. What have the spies who went to Jericho become convinced of after their interaction with Rahab, something they may or may not have been convinced of before?

6. Read Joshua 3. In this chapter the Israelites experience a repeat of something their parents experienced forty years before. What is it?

7. The ark of the covenant was the gold box that held the Ten Commandments. It was usually in the Most Holy Place of the tabernacle. What message do you think the ark of the covenant leading the procession communicated to the people crossing the dry river bed into Canaan?

Conquering the Land

8. Read Joshua 5:1–9. Abraham's descendants were about to enter into the land that had been promised to Abraham, but they had not taken upon themselves the sign of the covenant with Abraham's God, the sign

of circumcision. What impact do you think this nationwide circumcision would have had on the people?

9. Read Joshua 5:10–12. Think through the significance of Passover (look back at Exodus 12, if necessary). What would this celebration have impressed upon them as they prepared to inherit the land?

10. Read Joshua 5:13–15. What clues do you find in this passage to the identity of the commander of the army of the Lord?

11. What does the appearance of the commander of the army of the Lord with his sword drawn say about who is going to ensure victory in the battles ahead?

12. Read Joshua 6:1–16. This is a very unusual battle strategy. What do you think this would have communicated to Israel and to the other tribes in Canaan about what could be expected in the future?

13. Read Joshua 6:17–21, 24 along with Deuteronomy 20:16–18. How does the passage in Deuteronomy help us to understand the instructions of Joshua and the actions of Israel in the Joshua passage?

14. Read Joshua 11:16–23. What accomplishment do these verses summarize?

Inheriting the Land

15. Skim the headings of chapters 13–21. What process do these chapters describe in detail?

16. A pattern emerges in chapters 13–17 that hints at trouble ahead. What is it? (See 13:13; 15:63; 16:10; 17:12–13.)

Keeping the Land

17. Two great gatherings of God's people bring Joshua's life, this book, and this crucial period of conquest to a close. List three specific commands Joshua gave to Israel in chapter 23:1–13.

18. What sobering warning does Joshua give in 23:14–16?

19. In Joshua himself and throughout the book of Joshua, we see shadows of the greater Joshua who will come in the person of Jesus, the greater battle he will win, and the greater inheritance he will provide for his people. For each of the statements about Joshua in the first column below, write a corresponding statement about Jesus. Use the New Testament references for help and follow the examples provided.

Joshua	Jesus
Moses gave Joshua his name, which means "Yahweh saves." (Num. 13:16)	Matt. 1:21 *God instructed Joseph to give his son the name Jesus because, "he will save his people from their sins."*
God, to whom the whole earth belongs, charged Joshua to lead his people into Canaan to reclaim it for God, promising to be with him. (Josh. 1:2, 5)	Matt. 28:18–20 *Jesus, to whom all authority has been given in heaven and on earth, charged his disciples to go and make disciples of all nations, reclaiming people for God, promising to be with them.*
Joshua led the Israelites into physical battle against the people living in great wickedness in Canaan. (Deut. 18:10–14)	Eph. 2:2–3; 6:11–13
The ark going before the people signified that God himself was establishing his presence in the land among his purified people. (Josh. 3:3, 5)	John 14:2–3; Heb. 9:24

Joshua	Jesus
Joshua, led by the commander of the Lord's army, brought destruction against the enemies of God. (Josh. 5:13–15)	Rev. 19:14–15
Joshua brought divine judgment upon the Canaanites who persisted in wickedness and salvation to those who cried out for mercy. (Joshua 6)	Acts 2:21; 2 Pet. 3:9–10
Under Joshua, the Gibeonites, one small tribe of Gentiles, became part of the nation of Israel through faith in God's power and promise. (Joshua 9)	Rev. 5:9–10
The day came when the kings in Canaan became a footstool for the Israelites' feet, signifying complete defeat. (Josh. 10:24)	1 Cor. 15:25–28
Joshua impaled the bodies of the Canaanite kings on poles to demonstrate that they were under God's curse. (Deut. 21:22–23; Josh. 10:26)	Gal. 3:13

Joshua	Jesus
Joshua had the king's bodies taken down from the trees and put into caves and covered the openings with large stones that "remain to this day." (Josh.10:27)	Mark 16:4
Under Joshua, even after the Israelites entered into the land, perseverance in battle was required to take possession of all that God had given to them. (Josh. 11:18; 13:1)	Phil. 3:12–14
Joshua gave to each tribe the promised inheritance of land in the Promised Land of Canaan that they had been waiting for. (Joshua 13–21)	1 Pet. 1:3–5; 2 Pet. 3:13
Joshua brought the people to a place of rest. (Josh. 21:44)	Matt. 11:28; Heb. 4:8–9
Joshua called the people of God to loyalty to the Mosaic covenant so that they would not forfeit their promised inheritance of the land of Canaan. (Josh. 23:6–13)	Heb. 9:15

Teaching Chapter

There's No Place like Home

I don't remember a lot about my fourth-grade year at David Brewer Elementary School. But I do remember that we studied all about Australia, and we learned to sing all of the songs from *The Sound of Music*. I remember that when my teacher, Mrs. Lawrence, was mad, she would throw erasers across the room. And I remember that we did our own production of *The Wizard of Oz*. In fact, I will have you know that I had the role of Dorothy in the David Brewer Elementary School fourth-grade production of *The Wizard of Oz*. However, I should probably also tell you that I was not the first-string Dorothy. I was second string—not an understudy, mind you, as we second stringers performed the whole play, too, for the younger kids at the school; however, I can't quite say that I had the starring role. But I'm not bitter about it. Really. Okay, maybe a little.

In *The Wizard of Oz*, Dorothy has been taken away in her unconscious state to the Land of Oz, and from the minute she gets there, she wants to go home. The story takes us down the yellow brick road, through fields of poppies and skies of flying monkeys and into the Emerald City to see the great and powerful wizard. At the end, Dorothy discovers that all she really needed to do to get home was to click her ruby slippers together and begin to chant, "There's no place like home . . . there's no place like home . . ." When she does, she awakens back in her black-and-white world of Kansas prairie and says, "If I ever go looking for my heart's desire again, I won't look any further than my own backyard."

Have you ever given much thought to what the real message is of *The Wizard of Oz*? I think it's that there is really no better reality out there to long for—that the best place you and I can and should hope for is the here and now around us on this earth. But isn't there something inside us that knows that isn't true? Do you ever find in yourself a deep-seated discontent with life in this world as we know it, a sense that you were made for more? Well, you were. And in one sense, this is the story of the Bible from beginning to end. You and I were made to live with God's people in God's land under God's righteous rule. And the Bible is the story of God's wise working out of his plan to bring us into his holy land where we will finally be at home in his loving presence.

Eden: God's Land Established

One small stretch of real estate . . . will serve as a launching pad for his gospel of grace for sinners to spread to every corner of his creation.

In the garden of Eden, God's people—Adam and Eve—lived in a land that was created by and entrusted to them by God. In this land, all of their needs were met, and they had lives filled with purpose, enjoying perfect fellowship with the God who walked with them in the cool of the day. But Adam and Eve were expelled from this land of blessing because of their disobedience. They were sent away with the promise that a descendant would one day be born who would put an end to the misery brought into God's land by sin (Gen. 3:15). From Genesis 3 forward, the Bible is the story of God working out his plan to redeem and restore his people to his land, a land made holy by his very presence, a renewed paradise where he will live forever with them. But this plan will not come about in one instantaneous act. Instead, God will accomplish his plan beginning with one small stretch of real estate in which he will do a special work of redemption that will serve as a launching pad for his gospel of grace for sinners to spread to every corner of his creation. From a narrow land bridge that connects the continents of Africa, Europe, and Asia, God's covenant blessing will extend to the entire world. This plan began with one man, Abraham, whom God called out of Ur to go to the land God intended to give him.

> Now the LORD said to Abram, "Go from your country and your kindred and your father's house to the land that I will show you. And I will make of you a great nation, and I will bless you and make your name great, so that you will be a blessing. I will bless those who bless you, and him who dishonors you I will curse, and in you all the families of the earth shall be blessed." So Abram went, as the LORD had told him. . . . When they came to the land of Canaan, Abram passed through the land to the place at Shechem, to the oak of Moreh. At that time the Canaanites were in the land. Then the LORD appeared to Abram and said, "To your offspring I will give this land." (Gen. 12:1–4, 6–7)

A while later God became more specific about the territory being promised:

> The LORD said to Abram, after Lot had separated from him, "Lift up your eyes and look from the place where you are, northward and southward and eastward and westward, for all the land that you see I will give to you and to your offspring forever. (Gen. 13:14–15)

Later, the promise was reiterated but with an ominous prophecy included:

> Then the LORD said to Abram, "Know for certain that your offspring will be sojourners in a land that is not theirs and will be servants there, and they will be afflicted for four hundred years. But I will bring judgment on the nation that they serve, and afterward they shall come out with great possessions. . . . And they shall come back here in the fourth generation, for the iniquity of the Amorites is not yet complete." (Gen. 15:13–14, 16)

So Abraham is going to have offspring who will leave the land God is giving to him and go to a land where they will become servants. And we know that this is exactly what happened when Jacob's sons went to Egypt for grain during a famine and eventually became slaves of Pharaoh. This prophecy also tells us something else that is significant. When Abraham's descendants come back four hundred years later to live in the land God has given to them, they are going to be God's instruments to execute his judgment upon the people living there who have despoiled his land through their unbridled wickedness, which God can be patient with for only so long. When God spoke this prophecy to Abraham, the evil of the Amorites living in Canaan had not yet reached the point of deserving an obliterating judgment. But one day it would. The day would come when Israel would drive out not innocent people who were being unjustly attacked and invaded but guilty people fully deserving the judgment of God, delivered by the people of God.

God's promise of the land was later reaffirmed to Moses when God called Moses to go to Egypt to demand that Pharaoh release his people:

> I have come down to deliver them out of the hand of the Egyptians and to bring them up out of that land to a good and broad land, a land flowing with milk and honey, to the place of the Canaanites, the Hittites, the Amorites, the Perizzites, the Hivites, and the Jebusites. (Ex. 3:8)

These various tribes were squatters and interlopers in the land of promise, and God was about to evict them. Their evil had become more and more egregious with each new generation as they worshiped their false gods through shameful sexual practices and even by throwing babies into the fire (Deut. 18:10–11). Imagine if there were a country today in which parents routinely threw their children in a fire pit as a sacrifice to some imagined god. There would be constant coverage on every cable news channel. Celebrities would line up to demand that the United Nations put an end to this evil. But no one was calling out for this evil to stop in this ancient setting except for God himself. In an age when there was no worldwide cry for justice, God was about to use his people to put an end to this great wickedness and cruelty.[1] Don't think for a minute that this was divinely sponsored genocide. It wasn't. This was divine justice. But before executing justice, God extended mercy to the Canaanites, giving them a four-hundred-year opportunity to turn away from their wickedness and toward him, while his people were kept in slavery in Egypt.

---

[1]This suggestion of how the modern-day world would respond to the terrible wickedness of the Canaanites is adapted from similar comments made by Paul Blackham in his sermon "How to Win a Battle" (All Souls Langham Place, London, February 15, 2004).

Canaan: God's Land Promised

As the book of Joshua opens, we find the people of Israel camped on the border of Canaan, the land God had promised to give to them, where they will finally be at home, the land where they will enjoy the abundance of God's blessing and rest from all of their enemies. They are preparing to cross the Jordan and enter in, led by Moses's successor, Joshua. Joshua was introduced to Bible readers long before this book that bears his name. Back in Exodus 33 we read about Moses and Joshua meeting with the Lord face-to-face in the tent of meeting. But there is an interesting detail we may have missed in that account.

> When Moses turned again into the camp, his assistant Joshua the son of Nun, a young man, would not depart from the tent. (Ex. 33:11)

Think about this. Evidently Joshua lingered in the tent of meeting in the presence of the visible Lord after Moses left. How must this have shaped his understanding of God, his love for God, and his confidence in God? Surely this experience made God's promise of his ongoing presence all the more tangible to Joshua, when Yahweh said to him:

> Just as I was with Moses, so I will be with you. I will not leave you or forsake you. Be strong and courageous, for you shall cause this people to inherit the land that I swore to their fathers to give them. (Josh. 1:5–6)

God has prepared and protected an inheritance for his people—the land—and Joshua is going to be the one who will cause them to enter in and enjoy their inheritance.

When we come to chapter 5 of Joshua, the presence of God becomes even more vivid than Joshua had experienced to that point. Joshua went to take a look at Jericho, the first city they would have to take possession of in the land. Perhaps he was taking in the high, fortified walls and wondering how God was going to enable the Israelites to break through them. Perhaps he was wondering how God would fulfill his promise to be with him as he had been with Moses in the pillar of cloud and fire. If so, he didn't have to wonder for long.

> When Joshua was by Jericho, he lifted up his eyes and looked, and behold, a man was standing before him with his drawn sword in his hand. And Joshua went to him and said to him, "Are you for us, or for our adversaries?" (Josh. 5:13)

Standing before him was a magnificent warrior with his sword drawn. But what Joshua didn't yet realize was that this warrior's sword was not drawn against him, or against Israel, but against the wickedness of the Canaanites. Their iniquity was now complete, and their day of judgment had arrived.

> "I am the commander of the army of the LORD. Now I have come." And Joshua fell on his face to the earth and worshiped and said to him, "What does my lord say to his servant?" And the commander of the LORD's army said to Joshua, "Take off your sandals from your feet, for the place where you are standing is holy." And Joshua did so. (Josh. 5:14–15)

Joshua may have been appointed by God to lead his people into the land, but now he has met the supreme Commander, not only of Israel but of a mighty angelic army, the hosts of heaven. God has come to carry out his own will, his own plan by his own hand. He has come to be the captain of Israel's salvation (Heb. 2:10).

This account of Joshua's encounter with this mysterious warrior brings to mind Jacob's encounter with the man at Peniel (Gen. 32:22–32), who wrestled with him until daybreak. It also reminds us of Moses's encounter with the burning bush (Gen. 3:1–4:17), where Moses was told to take off his sandals because he was standing on holy ground. Clearly Joshua understood who it was that he was standing in front of— God himself in human form, perhaps the preincarnate Christ. So he took off his sandals and bowed before him. Maybe Joshua had been thinking about how difficult the coming battle was going to be. Perhaps he had been formulating strategies for a long and difficult siege. If so, it was now becoming clear that this war was not going to be won through human strength or strategy.

> The LORD said to Joshua: "See, I have given Jericho into your hand, with its king and mighty men of valor." (Josh. 6:2)

God spoke as if the battle was already over because, in essence, it was. This victory would not be the fruit of Joshua's brilliant tactics or Israel's powerful army. It would be the work of God, the gift of God.

At this point in the story, let's stop for a minute and imagine what it must have been like for Jesus, as a young boy and then as a young adult, to read the book of Joshua. "Joshua" is the Hebrew version of the name translated as "Jesus" in Greek. When Jesus read this book, he was reading a book with his own name as the title, the book he would have called "Jesus." In this man Joshua, who bore his name centuries before him, Jesus saw the shape his own life would take, how he would lead his people into the rest that God had promised to provide, and how he will one day come again to bring judgment on all those who persist in living out their wickedness on God's land. Here, in the book of Joshua, we see the deliverance Jesus accomplished in shadow form. Yet when Jesus came the first time, he did not accomplish his great work of deliverance by *brandishing* the sword of God's judgment. Instead, he delivered us by *bearing* the sword of God's judgment. "He was pierced for our transgressions" (Isa. 53:5). The sword of God's wrath against sin was turned against Christ in order to reconcile to God those who were his enemies (Rom. 5:10; Eph. 2:11–14). Because Christ was pierced by the sword of God's justice, we can be sure that the sword of the Lord will never be turned against us but is always for us. And "if God is for us, who can be against us?" (Rom. 8:31).

Canaan: God's Land Delivered

Finally it was time for the people of Israel to enter into Canaan to receive their inheritance. But there was something that had to be done before they could move forward and make themselves at home. They had to do something the previous generation had neglected to do. They needed to be circumcised. Through circumcision, they identified themselves with God's covenant promise to Abraham to make his descendants into a great nation, living in the land of promise, becoming a blessing to the whole world. By circumcising their sons, the Israelites expressed their longing for a new heart for God as they took up residence in this new land. They demonstrated that they were putting their trust in God's promise to take the curse upon himself for their inability to live up to the covenant stipulations. Then they celebrated Passover, identifying themselves as people who have been redeemed by the blood of the lamb. Celebrating the Passover meal, they demonstrated that they were people who longed for the Lamb of God, who takes away the sin of the world.

Once the men had healed, they were ready to move forward. But the battle plan provided to Joshua by the divine Commander was unconventional to say the least:

> You shall march around the city, all the men of war going around the city once. Thus shall you do for six days. Seven priests shall bear seven trumpets of rams' horns before the ark. On the seventh day you shall march around the city seven times, and the priests shall blow the trumpets. And when they make a long blast with the ram's horn, when you hear the sound of the trumpet, then all the people shall shout with a great shout, and the wall of the city will fall down flat, and the people shall go up, everyone straight before him. (Josh. 6:3–5)

Ancient battles were characterized by noise—not only the sounds of clashing swords and horses' hooves but also the yells and chants of opposing armies seeking to intimidate one another with their bravado. But every day for six days the Israelites got up and marched around the walls of Jericho in absolute silence. The Canaanites inside the walls of Jericho must have felt a growing sense of dread over the six days of silent marching, sensing that something terrible was about to happen. And they were right to be afraid. Finally the seventh day came.

> So the people shouted, and the trumpets were blown. As soon as the people heard the sound of the trumpet, the people shouted a great shout, and the wall fell down flat, so that the people went up into the city, every man straight before him, and they captured the city. Then they devoted all in the city to destruction, both men and women, young and old, oxen, sheep, and donkeys, with the edge of the sword. (Josh. 6:20–21)

Here in the ancient book of Joshua, we have a picture of the way our greater Joshua will lead us into God's land at the end of human history— with a shout and the sound of trumpets. Paul writes:

> For the Lord Himself will descend from heaven with a *shout,* with the voice
> of the archangel and with the *trumpet* of God, and the dead in Christ will
> rise first. Then we who are alive and remain will be caught up together
> with them in the clouds to meet the Lord in the air, and so we shall always
> be with the Lord. (1 Thess. 4:16–17)

Canaan: God's Land Cleansed

Joshua provides us with a picture of the way Jesus, our greater Joshua,
will deliver judgment on that day when all who persist in wickedness
and unbelief will be "devoted to destruction." On that great and terrible
day when Christ comes again, all those who have rejected Christ's shed
blood and perfect righteousness as their only hope will suffer the same
fate as those who lived in Jericho. Rich and poor, great and small, young
and old, will face God's fury when the commander of the Lord's armies,
who led the armies of Israel to kill every inhabitant of Jericho, will bring
complete and final destruction upon the city of man. But this book that
paints the picture of divine judgment upon the Canaanites is also quick
to make sure that we see what happens to those who deserve judgment
but cry out for mercy.

> But Rahab the prostitute and her father's household and all who belonged
> to her, Joshua saved alive. And she has lived in Israel to this day. (Josh. 6:25)

Wait a minute. A prostitute and her family are the only people in
Jericho who were spared? Who is this woman, and why is she "saved
alive"? Joshua 2 tells the story of two spies sent to Jericho before the rest
of the Israelites crossed over into Canaan. They made their way to the
kind of place in town where an outsider might be able to go unnoticed
while gleaning information about the city—the home, or inn, of a prostitute named Rahab. But apparently their presence did not go unnoticed
as the king sent emissaries to Rahab's home who demanded that the
two spies be brought out. At that point Rahab had a difficult decision to
make. If she turned these two men over to the king, she would likely be
rewarded. If she hid them, she'd be committing treason against Jericho
and its king and, if discovered, would be put to death. But that is what
she did, the risk she took. Why would she do that?

Before the men lay down, she came up to them on the roof and said to
the men, "I know that the LORD has given you the land, and that the fear
of you has fallen upon us, and that all the inhabitants of the land melt
away before you. For we have heard how the LORD dried up the water of
the Red Sea before you when you came out of Egypt, and what you did to
the two kings of the Amorites who were beyond the Jordan, to Sihon and
Og, whom you devoted to destruction. And as soon as we heard it, our
hearts melted, and there was no spirit left in any man because of you,
for the LORD your God, he is God in the heavens above and on the earth
beneath." (Josh. 2:8–11)

Word had reached Canaan in regard to what Yahweh had done to
bring his people out of Egypt, through the Red Sea, and the victories he
had given them over anyone and everyone who stood in their way. This
made the Canaanites afraid of the Israelites, because they were afraid
of Israel's God. But evidently it did a deeper work in Rahab than merely
making her afraid. While the hearts of the rest of the people melted
into fear, Rahab's heart was melted into faith. She came to believe that
Yahweh was going to give the land to his people—something that the
people of Israel were having a hard time believing—and she wanted in
on God's grace and goodness.

The judgment on the Canaanite city of Jericho was horrific, but
someone was spared. It wasn't the most upstanding, most impressive,
most religious, or most important person. It was the person who believed what God said and sought to come under his promise of grace for
sinners. For *anyone* and *everyone* who seeks God's mercy while it may
be found, experiencing that mercy is not a possibility but a certainty.

Jericho was the first of many battles in what would be an extensive
military campaign that played out over many miles and over several
years. And when we come to the end of the book of Joshua, we see that
God's promise that Israel will possess the land has been fulfilled.

Thus the LORD gave to Israel all the land that he swore to give to their
fathers. And they took possession of it, and they settled there. And the
LORD gave them rest on every side just as he had sworn to their fathers.
Not one of all their enemies had withstood them, for the LORD had given
all their enemies into their hands. Not one word of all the good promises

that the LORD had made to the house of Israel had failed; all came to pass. (Josh. 21:43–45)

The Lord was faithful to fulfill his promises. And for a time, Israel basked in covenant blessing under Joshua. But sadly they did not obey God's command to devote all of the Canaanites to destruction. Instead, they made peace with some of them and began to intermarry with them. Over time, they began to adopt some of their pagan practices and worship their pagan gods. Eventually, as we will discover as we work our way through the historical books, Israel's disobedience caused them to be evicted from the land God had given to them. God fulfilled his promise to give them the land, and they forfeited it through disobedience. Eventually a small number of Israelites made their way back to the land of Canaan, but they never had the rest from their enemies God had given them before. Instead, they found themselves oppressed by a foreign power, longing for God to restore to them all they had lost, a place where they could be at home.

The Whole World: God's Land Expanded

The day finally came when God sent a new Joshua, a new leader, to lead his people into the abundance of all that God had intended to give his people all along. But interestingly, this Joshua had very little to say specifically about the land, which is somewhat surprising when we consider the typical Jewish hopes and expectations of the Messiah. In fact, Jesus said, "My kingdom is not of this world" (John 18:36). He spoke of a kingdom that was not tied to the soil of Canaan but would encompass the entire earth. This was hard for the Israelites of his day to grasp. In fact, it was still primary in the minds of the two disciples walking on the road to Emmaus after the crucifixion when Jesus appeared and began to walk along with them. They said about Jesus, not knowing it was Jesus they were speaking to, "We had hoped that he was the one to redeem Israel" (Luke 24:21). Their hopes were still anchored in the nation and land of Israel. They did not yet see that by Christ's life, death, and resurrection, he had accomplished the redemption of Israel. Jesus didn't seem to show a great deal of sympathy for their nationalistic or territorial hopes. Appearing to ignore the subject they were really interested in, Jesus began to work his way through the Old Testament scriptures explaining them not in terms of the future of the nation of Israel or the land of Canaan, but in terms of himself. "And beginning with Moses and all the Prophets, he interpreted to them in all the Scriptures the things concerning himself" (Luke 24:27).

Forty days later, even after he had spent those forty days helping them to understand that the Old Testament—including the book of Joshua—was most profoundly about him and the salvation he accomplished through his death and resurrection, his closest followers were evidently still stuck on when he would restore the land and the rest that their ancestors had known in Joshua's day. Immediately before Jesus ascended into heaven, "they asked him, 'Lord, will you at this time restore the kingdom to Israel?'" (Acts 1:6). In his response, Jesus sought to correct not only the disciples' idea about the timing of the restoration to come but more significantly what would be restored. He wanted them to adjust and enlarge the idea of the kingdom they had inherited from their Jewish upbringing into a much bigger and broader understanding of the kingdom of God.

> He said to them, "It is not for you to know times or seasons that the Father has fixed by his own authority. But you will receive power when the Holy Spirit has come upon you, and you will be my witnesses in Jerusalem and in all Judea and Samaria, and to the end of the earth." (Acts 1:7–8)

Now every person in whom Christ dwells by his Spirit is holy land.

The kingdom of God was no longer going to be primarily about the nation of Israel living in the land of Canaan. In fact it had never really been limited to that. Israel was established by God to be the seed, the starting point, for a kingdom that would encompass the whole earth. This is the geography of grace.[2] So instead of instructing his followers on how they could take back their country from the Romans, Jesus commanded them, "Go therefore and make disciples of

---

[2] I heard John Woodhouse use this beautiful phrase for the story of Joshua, attributing it to Graham Cole.

all nations" (Matt. 28:19). The "land, crafted by the One who shaped the continents, was designed from the beginning not as an end in itself, but as a means to the end of reaching the world with the gospel."[3]

No longer would the kingdom of God be defined by borders or bloodlines. Now it would be embraced through belief in Jesus Christ. No longer would it be confined to those who worshiped in Jerusalem. Now Jerusalem would become the launching pad for declaring the grace made available to people from every tribe, tongue, and nation. No longer would citizenship in God's kingdom come by birth to a Jewish mother or father. Now it was clear that it comes to all—Jew and Gentile—through the new birth by God's Spirit. Now every person in whom Christ dwells by his Spirit is holy land. The shadow of the land of Canaan as the place where God dwelled with his people, like so many other shadows in the Old Testament era, has fallen away. Its substance, a kingdom that is not of this world, remains.

The land promise hasn't been revoked or replaced; it has been transformed and expanded. All of those who put their faith in Christ alone will one day dwell in the land that Abraham evidently always understood as the true essence and intention of God's promise. The writer of Hebrews says of Abraham: "By faith he went to live in the land of promise, as in a foreign land, living in tents with Isaac and Jacob, heirs with him of the same promise. For he was looking forward to the city that has foundations, whose designer and builder is God" (Heb. 11:9–10). Abraham evidently saw through the promise of the land into its deeper reality. And the New Testament clearly tells us that in Christ we have everything that God promised to Abraham and his descendants—including the land. We dwell in the holy land now as we abide in Christ and make our home in him.

We dwell in the holy land now as we abide in Christ and make our home in him.

In a sense, Dorothy in the *Wizard of Oz* was right. There's no place like home. We don't know this by experience but by faith based on God's promise, because we haven't yet experienced our heavenly home. How-

---

[3] O. Palmer Robertson, *The Israel of God: Yesterday, Today and Tomorrow* (Phillipsburg, NJ: P&R, 2000), 29.

ever the day will come when our greater Joshua will lead us into this land. Christ will return as the commander of the Lord's armies, and with his sword he will devote to destruction all the evil that has invaded his land. We will finally take full possession of our inheritance in the true land of milk and honey. This will be the land we've always longed for, the land that Canaan was always pointing toward, the land where we will finally be at home.

Looking Forward

New Heaven and New Earth: God's Land Inherited

Oftentimes when we read the Bible we come upon long sections made up of lists or details that we find difficult to take interest in. Perhaps Joshua 12–21 is a bit like that. Much of this section details the allotment of land in Canaan given to each tribe and clan. But whenever we come to something in the Bible that we find confusing or seemingly irrelevant to us, there is most likely a treasure to be found in it if we will dig. And that is certainly the case with this section of the book of Joshua.

God told Joshua to "allot the land to Israel for an inheritance" to the various tribes and clans. And in these chapters we get the details of the inheritance of each tribe. For example, for the people of Naphtali we read:

> And their boundary ran from Heleph, from the oak in Zaanannim, and Adami-nekeb, and Jabneel, as far as Lakkum, and it ended at the Jordan. Then the boundary turns westward to Aznoth-tabor and goes from there to Hukkok, touching Zebulun at the south and Asher on the west and Judah on the east at the Jordan. The fortified cities are Ziddim, Zer, Hammath, Rakkath, Chinnereth, Adamah, Ramah, Hazor, Kedesh, Edrei, En-hazor, Yiron, Migdal-el, Horem, Beth-anath, and Beth-shemesh—nineteen cities with their villages. (Josh. 19:33–38)

Because we are unfamiliar with the ancient geography, this doesn't mean that much to us. But if we were familiar with these places and with these people, we could better imagine their sense of wonder as their tribe was given this huge amount of territory in the Promised Land. Likely the people of this tribe would have looked at each other and said, "All of this for us?"[4]

As we read through the records of the allotment of earthly land to God's people in Canaan, we are learning about the inheritance that is waiting for us in heaven. The gospel promises us an inheritance—not in the dust of Palestine but in the heavenly kingdom of God, the new heaven and the new earth, the land we will live in forever when Jesus returns and renews all things. These chapters in the book of Joshua give us a preview of what it will be like when our greater Joshua, Jesus, leads us into the eternal Promised Land. There we will inherit all that God has promised. Peter wrote:

> Blessed be the God and Father of our Lord Jesus Christ! According to his great mercy, he has caused us to be born again to a living hope through the resurrection of Jesus Christ from the dead, to an inheritance that is imperishable, undefiled, and unfading, kept in heaven for you. (1 Pet. 1:3–4)

In Christ we are set to inherit everything the land stood for in Old Testament Israel—security, blessing, and the presence of God. In fact, our inheritance is better than what was given to the twelve tribes by Joshua. Our Joshua has caused us to inherit not just a slice of land in the Middle East but the whole world, the entire renewed earth. And we need never fear being cast out of this land. Jesus was cast out for us when he took all of our disobedience upon himself on the cross. His perfect obedience to the law of God becomes ours by faith. His Spirit seals us for the day of redemption so that we will one day receive our promised inheritance.

One day our Joshua will stand in front of us, and he will read out the inheritance that will be ours in the new heaven and the new earth, and it will be better than we have ever dreamed of. Surely we will breathlessly say in response, "All of this for me?"

---

[4] I came to see the allotment of Israel as an inheritance as a picture of our allotment of heaven as an inheritance by listening to Richard Coekin's sermon "The Inheritance We Await" (Saint Andrews @ Seven, Wimbledon, UK, October, 19, 2008).

Discussion Guide

Joshua

Getting the Discussion Going

1. Imagine that you were one of the Israelites standing on the shores of the Jordon River at the beginning of the book of Joshua. You have been living in a tent in the wilderness ever since you were a child hearing about the land of milk and honey, and now you are getting ready to go into the land you will call home. But, of course, there is that business of first doing battle with the people who live there now. What do you think you might be looking forward to and what might you dread?

Getting to the Heart of It

2. Three times in Joshua 1:6–9, Joshua is told by God to be strong and courageous. Why do you think he needed to hear this repeated command, and what was the basis for his strength and courage?

3. Think through the events found in Joshua 5–6 (circumcision of all the males, celebrating Passover, Joshua meeting the Commander of the army of the Lord, marching around and then taking Jericho). How is this battle preparation, battle leadership, and battle strategy different from typical battle, and why is it so different?

4. What does the story of the complete destruction of Jericho, except Rahab and her family, tell us about God's judgment as well as God's mercy?

5. In our day, as the people of God, we do not take up arms to subdue our enemies. But we do have an enemy to fight. According to Ephesians 6:10–18 and 1 Peter 5:8–9, who is our enemy, and how do we fight?

6. Just as the Israelites inherited territory, we as believers have an inheritance awaiting us. What is our inheritance, according to the following verses, and how can we be sure we will inherit it? Matthew 25:34; Romans 4:13; 1 Corinthians 15:50; Ephesians 1:11–14; Colossians 1:11–13; 1 Peter 1:3–5.

7. Understanding that Joshua and Jesus are the same name, one in Hebrew and one in Aramaic, how do you think it would affect the way we read, understand, and teach the book of Joshua and the stories within Joshua if we were to call the book "Jesus" instead?

Getting Personal

8. The essence of the Christian life is knowing and trusting in the promises of God. It is desiring the inheritance that is being kept for us in heaven so that we don't expect so much from this world. Do you cherish the inheritance that is being kept for you in heaven? If so, what nurtures that, and if not, why do you think that might be?

Getting How It Fits into the Big Picture

9. The book of Joshua tells us how God brings his people into the kingdom of God. It is written about the earthly kingdom of God to help us understand how we enter into the heavenly kingdom of God. Work your way through the following statements as a group. How does each of the following statements about the experience of the Israelites tell us about our own experience of coming into the kingdom of God?

∼ The Israelites had to follow their leader, Joshua.

∼ The Israelites had to believe the promise that God was giving them the land.

∼ The Israelites were miraculously transferred across the river into Canaan.

∼ Though God gave them the land, they had to fight many battles against their enemies to take possession of it.

∼ The day came when they possessed the land and had rest from all of their enemies.

Judges

Personal Bible Study

Judges

The book of Joshua is a record of victory and conquest and rest. But in the book of Judges, things change radically for the Israelites. This book records Israel's failure and deterioration and distress. But they should not really be so surprised that they are in such difficulty. Joshua had given them clear instruction before his death about what they needed to do and what would happen if they did not do it.

1. Read Joshua 23:11–16 and briefly summarize Joshua's instruction and warning.

2. Read Judges 1:18–36 and 3:5. What is the problem after Joshua died, and what did it lead to?

3. Read Judges 2:1–5. What is God's response to this problem?

4. Read Judges 2:10–15, which sets the scene for the rest of the book of Judges. What does each verse tell you about Israel during this time?

    v. 10

    v. 11

    v. 12

    v. 14

    v. 15

5. Read Judges 2:16–23. What happened next in this repeated cycle, according to the following verses?

    v. 16

    v. 17

    v. 19

6. According to Judges 3:1–6, what good purposes did God have in this difficult period of Israel's history?

Before the period of the Judges, Israel was united under the strong central leadership of Moses or Joshua, but during the time of the judges, the tribes of Israel operated as a kind of confederation, with each tribe seeking to maintain its sovereignty. None of these judges ruled over the entire nation of Israel but over particular tribes and territories.

Rather than reading Judges as a chronological story, we have to read it as a series of snapshots taken over a period of two hundred to three hundred years in various geographical areas of Israel. From Judges 3:7 through the end of chapter 16, this book tells the stories of twelve judges that God sent to rescue his people when they sinned and then called out to him to save them. Some of the judges seem to have good character and hearts to serve God, but others of them seem to exhibit little character or love for God. You may want to read or skim chapters 3 through 16 to get the full picture of what these judges were like and what they did. Or you can read the verses indicated to glean the repeated pattern of what happened during this period.

7. Othniel

What is the problem? (3:7)

How did God respond? (3:8)

What happened? (3:9)

How did Othniel accomplish their deliverance? (3:10)

How did this period end? (3:11)

8. Ehud

What is the problem? (3:12)

How did God respond? (3:12)

What happened? (3:15)

How did Ehud accomplish their deliverance? (3:16–29)

How did this period end? (3:30)

9. Deborah and Barak

What is the problem? (4:1)

How did God respond? (4:2–3)

What did Israel do? (4:3)

How did Deborah accomplish their deliverance?
(4:4–24, esp. vv. 6 and 15)

How did this period end? (5:31)

10. Gideon

What is the problem? (6:1)

How did God respond? (6:1–5)

What happened? (6:6–7)

How did Gideon accomplish their deliverance? (7:19–25)

How did this period end? (8:28–32)

11. Jephthah

What is the problem? (10:6)

How did God respond? (10:7–8)

What did Israel do? (10:10)

How did Jephthah accomplish their deliverance? (11:29–33)

How did this period end? (12:7)

12. Samson

What is the problem? (13:1)

How did God respond? (13:1)

What did Samson do? (16:28)

How did Samson accomplish their deliverance? (16:25–31)

How did this period end? (16:31)

13. The last four chapters of Judges, chapters 17–21, form an appendix. They provide further examples of the corruption of the time and contain some of the most distasteful parts of the Bible. The book ends with Israel's having descended into a civil war. The writer of Judges states the problem and hints at the solution several times in these chapters. What is the problem, according to Judges 17:6; 18:1; 19:1; and 21:25?

14. What is the implied solution suggested in 21:25?

Teaching Chapter

Holding Out for a Hero

The movies offer us larger-than-life heroes, and we love them for it. Rocky. Superman. Indiana Jones. Hans Solo. Who doesn't want a hero to show up and save you when all seems lost? Music offers us some thoughts on heroes, too. In the words to the song "Holding Out for a Hero," which was first made popular in the 1980s version of the movie *Footloose*, we're told exactly what a hero needs to be. "He's gotta be strong, and he's gotta be fast, and he's gotta be fresh from the fight." A few years later, in the 90s, two divas also sang about heroes, but they seemingly stopped looking "out there" somewhere for a hero and found one closer to home. Whitney Houston sang that "everybody's searching for a hero; people need someone to look up to." And what was her answer when she didn't find anyone to fill that need? "So I learned to depend on me." Similarly, Mariah Carey sang about a hero who comes along with the strength to carry on, and who is this hero? "Look inside you . . . a hero lies in you." Certainly this is the message we are fed in our self-empowerment culture: Don't look for someone "out there" to save you. It's really up to you to save yourself.

The book of Judges shows us what a world looks like in which people look inside themselves rather than outside of themselves for the hero they are searching for. And it is not a pretty picture—it is dark and distressing, and frankly, sometimes disgusting. As the book of Judges unfolds, we witness abuse of power in the name of God, religious prostitution, assassination, gang rape, and dismemberment. The book of Judges is full of despicable people doing deplorable things. But in the middle of this darkness and distress, Judges also presents us with hope—hope that a hero will come along, a hero who is fresh from the fight, a hero not from inside us but from outside us. Judges helps us to see not only that we really do need a hero but also exactly what we need our hero to save us from.

We Need a Hero to Save Us from Our Incomplete Obedience

When the book of Judges opens, the people of Israel are looking for a leader, a hero who will lead them in battle to overcome the Canaanites who remain in the land. And the Lord appoints the tribe of Judah to take the lead, saying, "Judah shall go up; behold, I have given the land into his hand" (1:2). The report on their efforts in Judges 1 contains both good news of defeating and capturing their enemies and bad news of not getting the job done completely.

> And the LORD was with Judah, and he took possession of the hill country, but he could not drive out the inhabitants of the plain because they had chariots of iron. And Hebron was given to Caleb, as Moses had said. And he drove out from it the three sons of Anak. But the people of Benjamin did not drive out the Jebusites who lived in Jerusalem, so the Jebusites have lived with the people of Benjamin in Jerusalem to this day. . . . Manasseh did not drive out the inhabitants of Beth-shean and its villages. . . . Ephraim did not drive out the Canaanites who lived in Gezer. . . . Zebulun did not drive out the inhabitants of Kitron. (Judg. 1:19–21, 27, 29, 30)

Judges 1 continues with a long list of Israelite failures to take possession of the land that God had given to them. Seven times the writer pounds out the problem tribe by tribe: they "did not drive out the inhabitants." The Israelites were willing to coexist with the most wicked people on the planet. They thought they knew best, that something less than full obedience would be good enough. And incomplete obedience, though we want credit for effort, is really just disobedience.

Is there some area of your life in which you have assumed that grace permits you to settle for something less than full obedience to what God has clearly commanded? I'm not talking about an area in which you continue the fight against sin. I'm asking, is there an area in your life in which you've given up the fight and settled into something less, anything less, than complete obedience? Is there wickedness in your world that you are accommodating instead of eradicating? Can you see that God always provides the needed power to obey him fully, not just halfway?

Why is the partial obedience of the Israelites a problem? As we bring our modern-day sense of what it means to be a good citizen of the world to this story, we are tempted to think that they were actually doing right by the Canaanites to make peace instead of war. But this was a unique place and time in which God was establishing what he intended to be his kingdom on earth in Israel. This was to be the holy land where he would dwell with his people. And God knew that what began as toleration would descend into outright capitulation to a Canaanite way of life with no regard for Yahweh. What seemed reasonable would prove lethal. Living *among* the Canaanites would result in living *like* the Canaanites. And so what did God do? The same God who came to Joshua as the commander of the Lord's armies came again in the person of the angel of the Lord to speak to all the people of Israel.

> Now the angel of the LORD went up from Gilgal to Bochim. And he said, "I brought you up from Egypt and brought you into the land that I swore to give to your fathers. I said, 'I will never break my covenant with you, and you shall make no covenant with the inhabitants of this land; you shall break down their altars.' But you have not obeyed my voice. What is this you have done? So now I say, I will not drive them out before you, but they shall become thorns in your sides, and their gods shall be a snare to you." As soon as the angel of the LORD spoke these words to all the people of Israel, the people lifted up their voices and wept. (Judg. 2:1–4)

Here we see an example of one of the ways God judges again and again in the Bible and in our day: he gives people what they want (see Rom. 1:24–32). *You want to live among these wicked people? Fine. I will let you live among these people and experience the consequences of accommodating that kind of evil in your midst.* What the people needed was a hero who would save them from the incomplete obedience that threatened to trap them forever in a downward spiral.

We Need a Hero to Save Us from Our Ignorance

In the second chapter of Judges we have a second introduction to the book, which starts over again with where we left off at the end of the book of Joshua. It helps us to understand a little more about these people who have refused to drive out the Canaanites from their land.

> And the people served the LORD all the days of Joshua, and all the days of the elders who outlived Joshua, who had seen all the great work that the LORD had done for Israel. . . . And all that generation also were gathered to their fathers. And there arose another generation after them who did not know the LORD or the work that he had done for Israel. (Judg. 2:7–8, 10)

The generation who were small children when the Israelites walked away from Egypt and through the Red Sea had died. Gone too was the next generation who marched around Jericho for seven days and saw the walls fall down. And something terrible had happened as that generation died off—something we fear happening in our own families: the previous generation had failed to pass along a living faith to their children. This new generation had *heard* the stories about Yahweh and his powerful deliverance and guidance and provision, but they hadn't *experienced* it for themselves. This generation was much like our own—born into prosperity and fascinated with the search for spiritual meaning among the many options presented in the colliding cultures around them—but they saw reading, loving, and obeying God's Word as terribly old-fashioned and irrelevant.

All of us who are parents want the secret formula for passing along a living faith to our children, and we are frustrated that there is no formula. But surely our kids need more than to *hear* about how their parents have experienced God in the past or even in the present. Surely our children need to be *involved* in ongoing experiences of putting faith to the test. Yet most of us do everything we can to avoid situations in which our families are forced to depend on God as our only hope, our only supplier, our only security. But if the next generation is going to

know the Lord, they have to know more than Bible stories or even correct doctrine. They have to *experience* what it means to trust God to deliver on his promised help. Maybe we shouldn't always be so quick to be
our children's savior. Maybe we should be willing to allow our children
to experience needing God to come to the rescue and discovering how
he does that.

Without a clear vision of Yahweh's claim upon them, it was natural
for this new generation to pursue Canaanite deities. So how would they
ever be saved from the spiritual ignorance that relegated Yahweh to an
old-fashioned religion? Only if a hero came who would reveal God to
them in a personal, unmistakable way. How are we going to pass along
our faith to our children? Only as our hero works through his Word im-
planted in their minds throughout their lives to call them to trust him
with their lives, only as he captures their hearts, moving them from
knowing *about* God to truly knowing God.

We Need a Hero to Save Us from Our Idolatry

Spiritual voids simply do not stay empty but are filled with other
things, and so it was for this generation of Israelites. Their experien-
tial ignorance of God led to their abandonment of God and embrace of
other gods.

> And the people of Israel did what was evil in the sight of the LORD and
> served the Baals. And they abandoned the LORD , the God of their fathers,
> who had brought them out of the land of Egypt. They went after other
> gods, from among the gods of the peoples who were around them, and
> bowed down to them. (Judg. 2:11–12)

I wonder how you feel when you read that or *if* you feel something
when you read it. Just two chapters earlier, in Joshua 24, we read that
when the Israelites were told to choose whom they would serve, the
whole nation said, "We will serve the LORD." And here we read: "They
abandoned the LORD. . . . They went after other gods." This should cause
us to feel the way we feel when we hear the sad news that a friend we
witnessed taking her wedding vows has left her husband for another
lover. We feel sick about it and shake our heads, wondering how what

began with such love and beauty could have devolved into abandonment and alienation. That is how we should feel when we read that Israel has abandoned even a pretense of loving God. She is going all out after other gods. So who are these gods, and what did it entail for Israel to "go after" them?

Baal was the god of the land. For land deals and commerce, you needed a baal. Baal was also the god of fertility. So to get your crops to grow and your cows to have calves and your wives to have children, you needed to appease Baal. Or really it was more to coerce Baal by acting out in front of Baal what you wanted Baal to do. So you went to one of the temples dedicated to Baal and had sex with a temple prostitute, saying to Baal, in effect, "This is what we want you to do for us—give us fertility." So instead of trusting the living God to provide what they needed, the Israelites indulged themselves sexually in pursuit of what they thought they needed to make them happy. Likely they saw themselves as very enlightened people to be so open to alternate ways of being spiritual.

In a recent issue of *O, The Oprah Magazine*, Martha Sherrill wrote an article called "The Spiritual Revolution" in which she described the spiritual evolution of her generation:[1]

> Whenever I visit my cousins in California, where I grew up, I'm reminded what a spiritually adventurous group we are. There are a dozen or more of us spanning the baby boomer generation. We span the spiritual landscape, too. Having come from Christian grandparents—Catholic and various Protestant traditions—we are now all over the map. As my sister Anina says, "You know me. I'll look under any rock. And there isn't a spiritual practice I won't try." . . . While a couple of my cousins were drawn to the Book of Mormon, and another joined a mainstream Protestant denomination, most of us wandered into ancient Eastern traditions like Buddhism and Sufism. We've done visualizations and prostrations. We've counted prayers on mala beads. We've gone on compassion retreats, silent meditation retreats, and long-life empowerments. We've met with tarot card readers, mediums, and a guru with his own South Pacific island ashram.
>
> I used to feel embarrassed by our spiritual experimentation; it felt so hapless, so random. But on reflection, our explorations aren't so random

---

[1]Martha Sherrill, "The Spiritual Revolution," *O, The Oprah Magazine*, May 2008.

after all; they're linked by a unity of purpose, a common goal, which for lack of a better word I'll call authenticity. We're out to find an authentic experience or tradition, a way to live more passionately, profoundly, truthfully.

Later in the article Ms. Sherrill quotes Jerome P. Baggett, associate professor of religion and society at the Jesuit School of Theology at Berkeley, in regard to people who describe themselves as spiritual: "They're saying, 'Yes, I want to have a connection to the sacred, but I want to do it on my own terms—terms that honor who I am as a discerning, thoughtful agent and that affirm my day-to-day life.'"

"God on my terms." This could serve as a definition of idolatry. In three places in the book of Judges we read that in those days, "everyone did what was right in his own eyes." In other words, they redefined god as they chose, they pursued gods in ways that appealed to them. They put their own preferences about what a god worthy of worship should be like above God's revelation of himself through his Word. They allowed the Canaanite culture around them to shape their spiritual search.

God had made it clear that they were to drive the Canaanites completely out of the land, but it was easier to let them be than to drive them out. Besides, they were interesting; they knew how to have fun. Over time, they became just the neighbors down the street whose kids had grown up with their kids and married each other, and it just didn't seem like that big of a deal. But, of course, God had warned that if they did not drive the Canaanites out, the Canaanites would lure the Israelites away from their exclusive love relationship with Yahweh. Canaanite gods would turn their heads and their hearts away from the one true God. And this is exactly what happened.

We Need a Hero to Save Us from Our Enemies

Can you imagine a husband discovering that the wife he loves is sleeping with other men and simply shrugging his shoulders and not caring? Wouldn't that indicate that he really didn't love her in the first place? Throughout the Bible, God makes it clear that he loves his people with a passionate love, a jealous love. He cannot simply shrug off her rampant infidelity. He must take action—drastic action—to cause her to call out his name again. This is what we see again and again in Judges.

> They abandoned the LORD and served the Baals and the Ashtaroth. So the anger of the LORD was kindled against Israel, and he gave them over to plunderers, who plundered them. And he sold them into the hand of their surrounding enemies, so that they could no longer withstand their enemies. Whenever they marched out, the hand of the LORD was against them for harm, as the LORD had warned, and as the LORD had sworn to them. And they were in terrible distress. (Judg. 2:13–15)

Perhaps that doesn't seem to you like the loving thing to do. But Israel belongs to a God who is so deeply committed to his beloved that he is not above inflicting misery in order to awaken her to his love. God's purposes in this are not to harm her but to save her, not to destroy her but to preserve her, not to drive her away, but to draw her back to himself. And he will do this—again and again.

> Then the LORD raised up judges, who saved them out of the hand of those who plundered them. (Judg. 2:16)

God raised up a series of judges to save those whom he loved, judges who were able to save not by their natural know-how or strength but by the strength he supernaturally provided. The middle section of the book of Judges tells the stories of a dozen of these judges. Now when we think of judges, we think of men and women in courtroom robes enforcing laws and enacting penalties. But these judges were not so much legal authorities as they were military leaders. (Think less like Judge Judy and more like Jack Bauer.) They were deliverers, saviors, and rescuers, raised up by God himself. And, frankly, they're an interesting lot. Some of them had stellar personal character, but many of them seem wholly lacking in it. All in all, they were significantly flawed heroes— one woman and eleven men in whom we see cowardice, presumption, lust, and violence.

We're used to looking for heroes in the Bible whom we can use as examples of character and conduct, so we don't really know what to do with Ehud's brutal assassination and Gideon's laying out a fleece and Jephthah's rash vow to sacrifice his daughter and Samson's chasing after women. But the point of recounting the stories of the judges is not to hold them up as examples of behavior. Instead, they are to be held up as trophies of God's grace. We are meant to see that God works through profoundly flawed people.

Don't we see the same thing in our day? Haven't you known people who have experienced great moral failures, who have personality defects and character flaws, even great doctrinal error? And yet we have to stand back and scratch our heads and admit that God is using them to advance his kingdom in a particular territory. There's a part of us that doesn't like it. We rightly have high standards for those who lead. But can you see what good news it is that God uses profoundly flawed people for his salvation purposes? It means that he can use you, and he can use me.

In fact, we read about these flawed judges in Hebrews, in the chapter that is all about people in the Old Testament who lived by faith:

> And what more shall I say? For time would fail me to tell of Gideon, Barak, Samson, Jephthah, of David and Samuel and the prophets—who through faith conquered kingdoms, enforced justice, obtained promises, stopped the mouths of lions, quenched the power of fire, escaped the edge of the sword, were made strong out of weakness, became mighty in war, put foreign armies to flight. (Heb. 11:32–34)

The judges were far from perfect saviors. And, really, that is the point. A better savior was needed.

When we read the stories of Gideon, Barak, Samson and Jephthah, we don't really come away thinking of them as people of great faith. Perhaps that's because we want people noted for faith to also be paragons of consistency in their living out of that faith. Yet aren't we people who seek to live by faith but struggle with enormous blind spots, embarrassing moral failures, a general lack of sound judgment, a lust for sex and for acclaim, and a great fear that God will not show up in the way he has promised? The judges simply brought no lasting change. While they were able to bring about change in the circumstances of the Israelites in terms of relieving oppression, they had no power to change the heart. In fact, under their leadership, things really only went from bad to worse.

We Need a Hero to Save Us from Our Increasing Corruption

In the pages of Judges we witness the relentless regress of the people of God from the heights of victory and rest when they entered the land under Joshua to the depths of chaos at the end of the period of the judges. At the beginning of the book of Judges we're given a preview or summary of the pattern that is going to take shape as we're introduced to various judges.

> Whenever the LORD raised up judges for them, the LORD was with the judge, and he saved them from the hand of their enemies all the days of the judge. For the LORD was moved to pity by their groaning because of those who afflicted and oppressed them. But whenever the judge died, they turned back and were *more corrupt* than their fathers, going after other gods, serving them and bowing down to them. They did not drop any of their practices or their stubborn ways. (Judges 2:18–19)

The same pattern repeats itself seven times in the book of Judges: the people are at rest in the land, then they rebel against God in idolatry, then God sends their enemies against them in judgment so that they cry out to God, then God rescues them by sending a judge to save them, and then they are at rest once again. But this is not merely a circular pattern.

Far more than a series of stories about flawed heroes, Judges is the story of a merciful God who is patient toward repeat offenders who are stubbornly resistant to him.

It is a downward spiral. Every cycle begins with the same statement or a variant of it: "And the people of Israel did what was evil in the sight of the Lord." Tolerated evil is not static in our lives; it is progressive. It keeps claiming more territory in our attentions and affections. It keeps taking more and more away from us even as we are fooled into thinking it is adding to our lives.

But even as Judges makes us uncomfortably aware of the increasing corruption of God's people, it serves to magnify the abundant grace of the people's God. Yahweh's grace is far more tenacious than his people's depravity. God keeps showing up to save people who repeatedly sabotage their own security. He has patience with people who refuse to learn from their mistakes. Only Yahweh loves this way. And so we must see that far more than a series of stories about flawed heroes, Judges is the story of a merciful God who is patient toward repeat offenders who are stubbornly resistant to him. God sends a savior to people who are so caught up in their wickedness that they love their sin more than they love the one who is saving them. But he still sends the savior. In fact, here in the Old Testament we see the principle Paul spelled out to the Romans: "Where sin increased, grace abounded all the more" (Rom. 5:20).

We Need a Hero to Save Us from Our Inadequate Repentance

Repeatedly, when their increased corruption brought about the misery it always does, the Israelites cried out to the Lord in pain. But we cannot confuse this with genuine repentance. There is a difference between becoming sadly aware of your failure and being ready to do something about it, a difference between coming under conviction and coming away from our sin. Tears are not a requirement of, nor are they a dependable sign of, genuine repentance. Change is the dependable sign of real repentance. Yet God responded to the inadequate repentance of the Israelites in mercy, sending them a series of short-term saviors.

We Need a King to Save Us by Ruling over Us

It is important to know when reading through Judges that we are not reading a chronological story but getting snapshots of various judges whom God raised up over various tribes and territories, although not over the entire nation. In fact, that is really the heart of the problem, which is summed up in the final verse of the book:

In those days there was no king in Israel. (Judg. 21:25)

Moses and Joshua had exercised leadership over the nation as a whole. But they were gone, and Israel was now a loosely connected coalition of tribes with no national leader. There was no one at the helm to keep pointing them toward God and encouraging them to obey God's Word. God raised up the judges to deliver them and establish peace for a time, but then the judge would die, leaving behind no sustained dynasty, no lasting leadership, no preserving power. What they needed was a king—a good king—who would be a man whose heart would be much like God's own heart, a king who would lead them away from idolatry, away from this downward cycle of corruption and into true knowledge of God and heartfelt obedience to God. They needed a covenant-keeping king who was anointed by the Spirit, one who would lead in doing what was right in the Lord's eyes rather than doing what was right in his own eyes.

A short time later God temporarily and partially gave them just such a king when he put David on the throne. But David's sons did not follow in his footsteps, and they left God's people longing for a more perfect king. The people waited and looked for and longed for the savior-king God said he would raise up for them. And when John the Baptist, the forerunner to Jesus, was born, his father, Zechariah, by the power of the Holy Spirit, was able to see and celebrate that finally God was raising up this king, saying:

> Blessed be the Lord God of Israel,
>   for he has visited and redeemed his people
> and has raised up a horn of salvation for us
>   in the house of his servant David,
> as he spoke by the mouth of his holy prophets from of old,
> that we should be saved from our enemies
>   and from the hand of all who hate us. (Luke 1:67–71)

Jesus is the hero they had been holding out for, the King they had been waiting for, the King they needed. And he is the King we need. We need more than a human monarch who will watch over us in this world. We need a ruler who will rescue us from a world that is passing away. We need a king who will demand our total allegiance. Our Savior-Deliverer-King has come down to rescue and rule over us.

We Need a King to Make Us Right in God's Eyes

In that last verse of Judges, which begins, "In those days there was no king in Israel," we also discover what happens when we have no king ruling over us and what we need our king to do for us. Because Israel had no king:

> Everyone did what was right in his own eyes. (Judg. 21:25)

They thought they knew what was right. They went with their gut instead of going with God's clear and certain Word. I wonder, if you had challenged them about their trips to the temple of Baal and their building of Asherah poles, would they have even spiritualized their confidence in their ability to know what was right, by saying, "I have a peace about it"? My friend, we can never underestimate our power of self-deception in regard to our inner desires and motives. That is why we need something more than a sense inside ourselves. We need a word from outside ourselves. We need the plumb line of God's clear and certain Word to show us what is good and right. Just as Israel needed a godly king to lead them in doing right in the Lord's eyes, so do we.

But more than just a king who will show us what is right and lead us in doing what is right in God's eyes, we need a king who is good enough and powerful enough to *make* us right in God's eyes. And that is what Jesus has done. Our great deliverer was "handed over to die because of our sins, and he was raised to life to *make us right* with God" (Rom. 4:25 NLT).

In the end we see that all the inadequacies of the judges in the book of Judges serve to reveal to us the excellencies of our true Savior-Deliverer-King:

⁓ Ehud was a fearless warrior who had a message for the king of Moab that was delivered in the form of a sword thrust into his belly. Jesus, too is a fearless warrior who has "disarmed the rulers and authorities and put them to open shame, by triumphing over them" (Col. 2:15). How did he overcome the powers of darkness? Not by thrusting a sword into anyone but by being nailed to a cross and by having a sword thrust into his side.

⌒ Gideon said, "Please, Lord, how can I save Israel? Behold, my clan is the weakest in Manasseh, and I am the least in my father's house." (Judg. 6:15). But it was actually Gideon's weakness that made him the perfect person to accomplish God's purpose, which was to point to the greater savior whom God would send. To fight the greatest battle of all time, Jesus became weak. He became vulnerable to death. Under Gideon God reduced the number of troops needed to accomplish a victory over his enemies to only three hundred men. But eventually God reduced his fighting force to only one man. Paul writes that God defeated his enemy and made it possible for us to "live in triumph over sin and death through this *one man*, Jesus Christ" (Rom. 5:17 NLT).

⌒ In the final, climactic moment of Samson's life, Samson put his hands on the two center pillars that held up the temple to Dagon, the Philistine's god, where he was chained and being made a spectacle of mockery. To defeat the enemies of the people of God required the death of Samson, as "the dead whom he killed at his death were more than those whom he had killed during his life" (Judg. 16:30). In this way Samson foreshadowed our greater savior, Jesus. He too was handed over and bound by Gentile oppressors and mocked as helpless. He too accomplished the deliverance of God's people by his own death.

My friend, don't settle for a hero inside of you. You need a hero outside of yourself. Jesus is the only hero worth holding out for. He will deliver you from your enemies and replace your idolatrous heart with one that beats with love for him alone. He will make you right before God's eyes by covering you in his own righteousness. He will save you to the uttermost. He is a hero worth singing about.

> Give the winds a mighty voice: Jesus saves! Jesus saves!
> Let the nations now rejoice: Jesus saves! Jesus saves!
> Shout salvation full and free; highest hills and deepest caves;
> This our song of victory: Jesus saves! Jesus saves![2]

---

[2]Priscilla J. Owens, "Jesus Saves!"

Looking Forward

All Oppression Shall Cease

Unlike the people of God in the book of Judges, who were being oppressed by their enemies because of their disobedience and abandonment of God, the people of God in the book of Revelation are being oppressed and persecuted because of their obedience and faithfulness to God. But like the people of God in Judges, they are crying out to God.

> They cried out with a loud voice, "O Sovereign Lord, holy and true, how long before you will judge and avenge our blood on those who dwell on the earth?" (Rev. 6:10)

They long for God to send a warrior to fight against their enemies on their behalf, a judge who will set things right. They are holding out for a hero. And finally, he comes:

> Then I saw heaven opened, and behold, a white horse! The one sitting on it is called Faithful and True, and in righteousness he judges and makes war. His eyes are like a flame of fire, and on his head are many diadems, and he has a name written that no one knows but himself. He is clothed in a robe dipped in blood, and the name by which he is called is The Word of God. And the armies of heaven, arrayed in fine linen, white and pure, were following him on white horses. From his mouth comes a sharp sword with which to strike down the nations, and he will rule them with a rod of iron. He will tread the winepress of the fury of the wrath of God the Almighty. On his robe and on his thigh he has a name written, King of kings and Lord of lords. (Rev. 19:11–16)

Here is the true hero, the perfect judge that all of the judges in the book of Judges were pointing toward. Here is the King they did not have in their time, the King who will rule over all of those who have been made right in God's eyes. He will not only defeat all the forces of evil; he will also put a final end to the conflict. Every mechanism for tyranny conceived in the wickedness of the world will be thrown into the bonfire of God's grace.

As we live life in a world in which it seems as though evil often has the upper hand, and as we witness the persecution and oppression of many who identify themselves with Christ, this picture revealed in Revelation fills us with confidence that the day will surely come when the Hero we have held out for will come. This time he will not come in weakness but in strength. The blood of his enemies on his clothing will give evidence that he is fresh from the fight. No longer will people do evil in the sight of the Lord, as all evil will be banished. No longer will we devolve into greater and greater sin, as sin will be no more. No longer will we be oppressed by the enemies of God, as all of God's enemies will be destroyed.

It is not up to us to heroically overcome evil and oppression by our own strength or cunning. The true Judge of the earth will come. And when he comes, all oppression shall cease and the victory celebration will have only just begun.

Judges

Getting the Discussion Going

1. We didn't really spend time in the Personal Bible Study or Teaching Chapter on the colorful stories of some of the judges in Israel. What are some of your observations about these judges from reading this week or from hearing their stories in the past? *Samson be WILD*

Getting to the Heart of It

2. We've often heard some of these judges held up as heroes and have been encouraged to follow their examples. What do you think about that approach to the stories in the Old Testament, and specifically in Judges, at this point? *Probably not the best idea. They all had a weakness*

3. Read Hebrews 11:32. Knowing how flawed these judges were, how do you think they could be listed in this chapter of people who lived by faith? Does this offer us any insight or encouragement? *Same w/ us. Even w/ their flaws, saving faith is all they need*

4. The big cause of the people's problem during the days of the judges was their peaceful coexistence with sin shown in their unwillingness to obey God's clear instructions to devote the Canaanites to destruction. Read each of the following verses aloud in your group: Matthew 18:8–9; Romans 8:12–13; and Colossians 3:5. What do these verses say about how we are to deal with evil? *Kill evil in our lives*

5. Over and over again in Judges, we witness the people of Israel crying out to the Lord in their distress. Do you think their crying out to God was genuine repentance? Why or why not? *repentance requires turning away*

6. The last verse of Judges explains the reason there was so much evil in Israel during this time: everyone did what was right in his own eyes. Instead of obeying God's law and seeking to do what was right in God's eyes, they determined for themselves what was right and what was wrong, influenced significantly by the Canaanite culture around them. What do you think it takes to develop a desire for and to have the ability to do what is right in God's eyes? *pray, reading + community*

7. Judges is a hard and dark book of the Bible. Did you find any hope in it? Did you see any glimmers of grace? *the land had rest   all leading to ultimate judge*

Getting Personal

8. While the judges God raised up had the power to save Israel from her political oppressors, they had no power to save the people from the oppression of their incomplete obedience, their ignorance of God, their idolatrous ways, or their inner corruption. While the judges brought about a temporary change in people's circumstances, they were never able to bring about a change in people's hearts. As we worked our way through the various things we need to be saved from, was there one that struck a particular chord with you? *sexual indulgence, lust, harmony*

Getting How It Fits into the Big Picture

9. Judges is a bridge book in between the leadership of Moses and Joshua over Israel and the establishment of the monarchy under Saul and then David. Throughout Judges God sends delivers and saviors who deliver but are tremendously flawed. And the salvation they accomplish doesn't last. How do you think the book of Judges points readers toward Christ? *how we need the ultimate judge*

Week 4

Ruth

Ruth

1. In Ruth 1:1 we discover the setting for the story that makes up this short book. The events recounted took place "in the days when the judges ruled." What were those days like, according to last week's lesson?

2. Read Ruth 1:1–4 and summarize in a sentence or two what has taken place.

3. According to Ruth 1:8, what has happened that offers hope in what seems a hopeless situation for Naomi?

4. Read Ruth 1:7–18. Note the difference in what the two daughters-in-law did along with what you think motivated each to do what they did.

5. Read Ruth 1:19–21. How would you describe Naomi and her assumptions about her circumstances?

6. Most of us have heard Ruth's words before, often used in the context of a wedding service. But something more significant than family commitment is taking place here. What is it?

7. Read Ruth 2:1–16. What was it that Ruth expected and found when she went out to the fields (vv. 2, 10, 13)? List several examples of what she experienced.

8. Read Ruth 2:17–20. What does Naomi realize about the field where Ruth has gleaned?

9. What is the role of a family redeemer, according to the following verses from the law of Moses?

Deuteronomy 25:5–6:

Leviticus 25:23–28:

10. Read Ruth 2:23–3:9. When Ruth goes to Boaz informing him that he is a redeemer, what is she asking of him, according to the Deuteronomy and Leviticus passages above?

11. Read Ruth 3:10–17. What was Boaz's response to Ruth's request?

12. Read Ruth 4:1–13. How did Boaz follow through on his stated intentions?

13. Read Ruth 4:16–22. How do these final verses provide the primary reason for which the Bible tells us this story of one family living during the time of the judges?

14. Read Matthew 1:1–6, which provides the genealogy of Jesus. Mostly this genealogy is a list of fathers. But there are three mothers included in this section. Who are they and what do they have in common?

15. In the person and work of Boaz, we see shadows of the greater redeemer who will come in the person of Jesus, the greater price he will pay, and the greater redemption he will accomplish. For each of the statements about Boaz in the first column below, write a corresponding statement about Jesus, helped by the New Testament references provided, if needed.

Boaz as Redeemer	Jesus as Redeemer
Boaz was a relative of those in need of redemption. (Ruth 2:1)	John 1:14; Heb. 2:17 *Jesus was made a flesh and blood brother to those in need of redemption.*
Boaz was a worthy (or wealthy) man who shared his wealth with those he redeemed. (Ruth 2:1)	2 Cor. 8:9
Boaz came from Bethlehem. (Ruth 2:4)	Matt. 2:1
Boaz commended the faith of a foreigner. (Ruth 2:11)	Matt. 15:21–28
Boaz invited a foreigner to eat with him at his table. (Ruth 2:14)	Luke 14:15–24

Boaz as Redeemer	*Jesus as Redeemer*
Boaz fed Ruth until she was satisfied with some left over. (Ruth 2:14)	Luke 9:17
Boaz was determined to redeem and would not rest until it was accomplished. (Ruth 3:11, 13)	John 4:34; 19:30
Boaz paid the price of redemption outside the city gate. (Ruth 4:1)	Heb. 13:12
Boaz paid the cost to accomplish redemption. (Ruth 4:9–10)	1 Pet. 1:18–19
Boaz's redemption made it possible for Ruth, a foreigner, to be included in God's people by grace through faith. (Ruth 4:11)	Gal. 3:13–14

Teaching Chapter

Fields of Grace

Most of us have seen the opening shot of a movie or television show that begins with a picture of the earth hanging in space and then slowly zooms in, getting closer and closer, eventually focusing in on one city, one house, even one person. This is the wonder of long-range imaging technology. Using this technology, a camera out in space can zoom down beneath the ocean's surface to explore an ancient shipwreck or see into enemy territory to reveal where troops are moving. In fact, if you want, Google Earth will enable you to create a video that begins thousands of miles above the earth and then slowly zooms in to your address, down to an image of your dog sleeping in the sunshine on your back deck.

If we were to view the geography of the Bible through satellite imagery, beginning in Genesis 1 we would first see the entire earth with its land separated from its seas. As we made our way through the first few books of the Bible, the picture would slowly zoom in on the land bridge that connects the continents of Africa, Asia, and Europe. It was on this strip of Middle Eastern real estate that God chose to launch his work to redeem the whole earth.

So far in this study of the Old Testament historical books, the zoom on the satellite lens has gone just as far as to encompass this territory, assigned by Joshua to the twelve tribes. We can see the arid deserts in the south, the coastal plains, and the central mountain range. The green vegetation that is abundant at the headwaters of the Jordon in northern Israel stands out to us and extends along the edges of the Jordan River, going south toward the Sea of Galilee, becoming less and less fertile down to the Dead Sea. Via the book of Ruth, we now zoom in much closer, bringing into focus one little town in the Judean wilderness. But, in fact, we're going to zoom in even closer than that. We're going to zoom down into the fields surrounding Bethlehem, the fields inherited by one particular clan when they entered into the Promised Land under Joshua. In fact, we'll zoom down even further into the home of one ordinary Israelite family living in the town of Bethlehem, the home of Elimelech.

In the last lesson we got a wide-angle view of what was going on in the land in the years between the time when the Israelites moved in under Joshua and before they became united under a king. With no king to rule and guide them, everyone did what was right in their own eyes making it a time of cruelty and chaos. Certainly the people living in that time of misery who still gave any thought to God must have wondered if God had given up on his plan to use Israel as his chosen channel through which all the families of the earth were to be blessed (Gen. 12:3). The little book of Ruth, set in this time of the judges, lets us know that God had not given up on his plan but was, in fact, providentially guiding history to bring it about. Through this little ordinary family going through extraordinary difficulty, God was about to put on display how he would make a way for the people of God who had walked away from the grace of God to come home to it. And he was going to show how he would draw those who are strangers to his grace to become partakers in it. He was about to turn Bethlehem's fields of grain into fields of grace.

A Gracious Intention

The name of this little town, Bethlehem, means "house of bread." So on a satellite photo taken sometime in the mid-fourteenth or late thirteenth century BC, we might expect to see fields of grain waving in the wind around Bethlehem. But there is no grain. The fields of Bethlehem are dry and dusty. We read about it in the first verse of the book of Ruth.

In the days when the judges ruled there was a famine in the land. (Ruth 1:1)

There is no bread in the house of bread. Remember that this was supposed to be the land flowing with milk and honey. And instead there is a famine. God's intentions for his children are always to use whatever means possible to awaken us to his goodness, to call us back to himself. So this famine really reflects God's gracious intentions, though evidently Elimelech, the father in our family, cannot see it, or he refuses to see it. These were the days when "everyone did what was right in his own eyes," and evidently that is what Elimelech is doing.

> A man of Bethlehem in Judah went to sojourn in the country of Moab, he and his wife and his two sons. The name of the man was Elimelech and the name of his wife Naomi, and the names of his two sons were Mahlon and Chilion. They were Ephrathites from Bethlehem in Judah. They went into the country of Moab and remained there. (Ruth 1:1–2)

Instead of responding to the famine in repentance and waiting for God to work to relieve their suffering as he did again and again in the time of the judges, Elimelech decided he would save himself and his family. He determined to take them away from the one place on earth where God had promised to bless and dwell with his people, to a pagan land where the people worshiped pagan gods, the country of Moab, a people founded out of the incestuous relationship between Lot and his oldest daughter. This is where Elimelech decided to pin his hopes for his family and their future. Perhaps they left thinking it would be only temporary, but the writer says they "went into the country of Moab and remained there." And then tragedy struck. The family's pursuit of satisfaction and security away from God's place of blessing was a failure inscribed on gravestones in Moab.

> But Elimelech, the husband of Naomi, died, and she was left with her two sons. These took Moabite wives; the name of the one was Orpah and the name of the other Ruth. They lived there about ten years, and both Mahlon and Chilion died, so that the woman was left without her two sons and her husband. (Ruth 1:3–4)

First, Elimelech died, leaving Naomi a widow. She was an immigrant single mother in a place where she didn't speak the language or have any extended family. But at least she had her boys. The boys got married and settled down, and before they knew it, they'd been there ten years. And then both sons died—the sons Naomi had come to depend on since her husband had died—were gone. Naomi was left with two foreign daughters-in-law, who also were bereft. Days of happiness had become a distant memory.

And then, a glimmer of hope.

A Gracious Visitation

> She heard in the fields of Moab that the LORD had visited his people and given them food. (Ruth 1:6)

Grace came down to the fields outside Bethlehem. The Lord provided bread in the house of bread. Naomi was wooed by this grace to return to the place where she could experience it again.

> So she set out from the place where she was with her two daughters-in-law, and they went on the way to return to the land of Judah. (Ruth 1:7)

Ruth and Orpah headed out with Naomi as she set out toward Bethlehem. But at one point in the journey Naomi stopped and told the girls to head back to their own families. They were still young enough to find other husbands and have families of their own. If they went with Naomi to Israel, where they would likely be hated for being foreigners, there was little chance that they would find husbands and have a family. Besides, Naomi was sure that "the hand of the LORD has gone out against" her (Ruth 1:13), so she was trying to convince them that they couldn't expect to experience anything good in their future if they went with her. All three women were there in a heap in the middle of the road weeping. Orpah thought it through. She could go with Naomi, her aging, bitter mother-in-law, and have Naomi's God but likely little else. Or she could go home to her family and their gods where she would more likely be able to marry again and have children and enjoy acceptance. If she were to go home, she would have everything the world has to offer minus Jehovah. And that was her choice. Ruth, however, came to a different conclusion.

But Ruth said, "Do not urge me to leave you or to return from following you. For where you go I will go, and where you lodge I will lodge. Your people shall be my people, and your God my God. (Ruth 1:16)

When we hear those words, there is something about them that sounds familiar (and not just that we've heard them read out of context at a thousand weddings). Back in Genesis God had told Abraham:

And I will establish my covenant between me and you and your offspring after you throughout their generations for an everlasting covenant, to be God to you and to your offspring after you. (Gen. 17:7)

And when he brought his people out of slavery in Egypt, God had said to them:

I will take you to be my people, and I will be your God, and you shall know that I am the LORD your God, who has brought you out from under the burdens of the Egyptians. (Ex. 6:7)

Here was Ruth, who had grown up in a land and a family where there was no knowledge of the one true God and his promise to bless. Then she married a man who told her of the God who made promises to his forefathers and redeemed his people out of Egypt and brought them into a good land.

> *Ruth, a foreigner to the people of God, a stranger to the promises of God, has taken hold of them and made them her own.*

These were the promises she had married into, and she did not want the death of her husband to be the death of her hope. Ruth seemed to understand that the God of Israel gives grace to anyone who will turn to him and embrace him by faith. Her confidence in the covenant-making, covenant-keeping God of Israel emboldened her to abandon all of her previous sources of security. So she literally walked away from her identity as a daughter of Moab to become a daughter of the covenant community of Israel. When we hear her say, "Your people shall be my people, and your God my God," we are listening to a confession of personal conversion. Ruth, a foreigner to the people of God, a stranger to the promises of God, has taken hold of them and made them her own.

A Gracious Provision

When Naomi and Ruth arrived in Bethlehem, they discovered that what they had heard was really true, as it was "at the beginning of barley harvest" (Ruth 1:22). God had visited his people and they were reaping the harvest of his gracious provision. There was, however, no crop to be harvested on Elimelech's old, abandoned property and no money to buy food. Perhaps Ruth and Naomi found what was left of the old mud hut in Bethlehem and slept in it that first night back in town. But then they woke up hungry. It was a desperate situation. But it was not completely hopeless. God had made a provision for those in just such dire straights in his law. Back in Leviticus we find the record of God's instructions to Israel:

> When you reap the harvest of your land, you shall not reap your field right up to its edge, neither shall you gather the gleanings after your harvest. And you shall not strip your vineyard bare, neither shall you gather the fallen grapes of your vineyard. You shall leave them for the poor and for the sojourner: I am the LORD your God. (Lev. 19:9–10)

Ruth had learned about this gracious provision from God for the poor. So that first morning she headed out the door to gather whatever grain she could find on the edges of the fields where harvesters were at work. In our modern setting, Ruth would be the immigrant living in a cardboard box under the bridge heading out early in the morning to search for aluminum cans in hopes of collecting enough to cash in to buy dinner. Ruth likely could not have expected a glad welcome at the edges of the field. The Moabites had, only a short time before, enslaved the Israelites for eighteen years. It was a king of Moab who hired Balaam to curse the tribes of Israel. So surely the poor of Israel would not appreciate a Moabitess picking up what little grain they hoped to gather at the edges. But while Ruth may have been aware of what she might encounter, she didn't head out the door expecting abuse. Instead, she headed out the door expecting to find grace.

> And Ruth the Moabite said to Naomi, "Let me go to the field and glean among the ears of grain after him in whose sight I shall find favor." (Ruth 2:2)

Ruth put her confidence in the one who had said, "I will be your God and you will be my people," so her expectation was to find favor, or grace, in fields of grain.

> So she set out and went and gleaned in the field after the reapers, and she happened to come to the part of the field belonging to Boaz, who was of the clan of Elimelech. (Ruth 2:3)

The writer of the book of Ruth is having a bit of fun with us here when he writes that Ruth just "happened" to end up on the field of one of her late father-in-law's relatives. This hasn't just happened. It wasn't blind luck or coincidence that brought her to this particular field; it was the providential hand of God. Something bigger is happening here than just a hungry girl gleaning. God is working out his plan for his people. He is bringing a foreigner into the family.

> And behold, Boaz came from Bethlehem. And he said to the reapers, "The LORD be with you!" And they answered, "The LORD bless you." (Ruth 2:4)

Here is evidence that Boaz is an exceptional man in his day—a day in which men did what was right in their own eyes with little thought of God. Just by his greeting he shows that he is a man walking in the covenant promises God made to be with his people. The Lord of steadfast kindness is on

His heart was moved by the grace of his God who has always called people from every tribe and nation to be grafted into the olive tree of Israel.

his mind and on his lips. Boaz asks who the young woman is who is picking up grain along the edges, and his foreman tells him that she is the Moabitess who returned with Naomi and that she has been working hard in the fields since early morning.

> Then Boaz said to Ruth, "Now, listen, my daughter, do not go to glean in another field or leave this one, but keep close to my young women. Let

your eyes be on the field that they are reaping, and go after them. Have I not charged the young men not to touch you? And when you are thirsty, go to the vessels and drink what the young men have drawn." (Ruth 2:8–9)

Ah, there it is—grace, unmerited favor. Grace even more abundant and more amazing than Ruth could have expected. Instead of referring to her as "the Moabitess," which would have emphasized her outsider status, Boaz calls her "my daughter," taking responsibility for her. He wants to provide for her, protect her. He's heard all about how she has bound herself to her mother-in-law at great cost to herself and also how she has bound herself to Yahweh. Perhaps he remembered that Abraham himself was a foreigner and a stranger to the land of promise, that he too was one who had served other gods and left his family, turning his back on their gods, and putting his faith in the one true God who had called him out of that far-off land.

Or perhaps Boaz was thinking of his own mother. In the book of Matthew, when we read the genealogy of Jesus, we discover that Boaz's mother was Rahab the prostitute. His own mother was a foreigner to the promises of God and yet reached out and made them hers through faith. Perhaps when Boaz thought of his mother and looked into the eyes of Ruth, his heart was moved by the grace of his God who has always called people from every tribe and nation to be grafted into the olive tree of Israel. Boaz offered Ruth acceptance in the people of God. And Ruth was amazed by grace.

Then she fell on her face, bowing to the ground, and said to him, "Why have I found favor in your eyes, that you should take notice of me, since I am a foreigner?" But Boaz answered her, "All that you have done for your mother-in-law since the death of your husband has been fully told to me, and how you left your father and mother and your native land and came to a people that you did not know before. The LORD repay you for what you have done, and a full reward be given you by the LORD, the God of Israel, under whose wings you have come to take refuge!" (Ruth 2:10–12)

Here is the beautiful picture, laced throughout the Bible, of God as a mother hen who spreads her wings over her little chicks to draw them in close and protect them from harm. And Boaz is not finished showing grace to Ruth. He tells his men to let her glean, not just on the edges but in the heart of the fields where the grain is abundant. So by the time she heads home, she has at least 30 pounds of barley. Now, think about a 5-pound bag of flour and imagine wrapping up six or seven of those 5-pound bags in your big scarf and hauling them home on your back. It would make a statement when you staggered in the door. And Naomi, who has been able to think of little else than her empty stomach and her empty heart all day long, sees her daughter, who went out empty-handed, come through the door with a sack full of grain.

> And her mother-in-law said to her, "Where did you glean today? And where have you worked? Blessed be the man who took notice of you." So she told her mother-in-law with whom she had worked and said, "The man's name with whom I worked today is Boaz." (Ruth 2:19)

And this name rings a bell with Naomi. Boaz. You can almost see the light coming on and the wheels beginning to turn in her head.

> And Naomi said to her daughter-in-law, "May he be blessed by the LORD, whose kindness has not forsaken the living or the dead!" Naomi also said to her, "The man is a close relative of ours, one of our redeemers." (Ruth 2:20)

By "one of our redeemers," Naomi means that because Boaz is a close relative, he could fulfill the role of kinsman-redeemer as provided for in the law God gave to Moses. A redeemer acted as protector, de-fender, avenger, or rescuer for other members of the family, especially in situations of threat, loss, poverty, or injustice. When a family member fell into poverty and had to sell his land, the kinsman-redeemer could buy it back and restore it to the family so that it stayed within the family. And when a family member died without an heir, the kinsman-redeemer could marry the widow with the aim of producing an heir, not for himself but for the dead husband. So when Naomi heard about the close relative, Boaz, who was so kind to Ruth, she wondered if Boaz might be willing to serve as kinsman-redeemer to provide an heir to inherit the land that once belonged to Elimelech. Of course, she was too old to marry and have children. But Ruth was not.

A Gracious Redemption

So Ruth continued to glean in the fields of Boaz throughout the summer. When the season of harvesting came to an end, the men were so busy threshing the harvested grain that they didn't even go home to sleep at night but just slept on the threshing floor. And Naomi decided it was time to take action. Naomi instructed Ruth to wash and perfume herself and sneak onto the threshing floor under cover of darkness and lay down at the feet of Boaz.

> So she went down to the threshing floor and did just as her mother-in-law had commanded her. And when Boaz had eaten and drunk, and his heart was merry, he went to lie down at the end of the heap of grain. Then she came softly and uncovered his feet and lay down. (Ruth 3:6–7)

Boaz wakes up because his feet are cold. But when he goes to tuck in the covers around his cold feet, he makes a startling discovery.

> At midnight the man was startled and turned over, and behold, a woman lay at his feet! He said, "Who are you?" And she answered, "I am Ruth, your servant. Spread your wings over your servant, for you are a redeemer." (Ruth 3:8–9)

Notice that she uses the same phrase Boaz had used when he first met her and prayed for blessing on this one who had taken refuge under the wings of the God of Israel (Ruth 2:12). In a sense, Ruth is asking Boaz to be the answer to his own prayer. She's saying, "Cover me. Redeem me. Take me from foreigner to family, from widow to wife, from one without provision, protection, or privilege to one who shares your abundance, safety, and rest."[1] She is really saying, "Will you marry me?" And immediately we sense Boaz wants to. Boaz says:

> May you be blessed by the LORD, my daughter. You have made this last kindness greater than the first in that you have not gone after young men, whether poor or rich. And now, my daughter, do not fear. I will do for you all that you ask. (Ruth 3:10–11)

---

[1]David Helm, "Ruth 2," sermon (Holy Trinity Church, Chicago, October 5, 2003).

She has an affirming yes, but there is a slight hitch.

> And now it is true that I am a redeemer. Yet there is a redeemer nearer than
> I. Remain tonight, and in the morning, if he will redeem you, good; let him
> do it. But if he is not willing to redeem you, then, as the LORD lives, I will
> redeem you. (Ruth 3:12–13)

There is a closer living relative to Elimelech who has the first rights
of refusal to serve as redeemer. So Ruth leaves. She knows she's engaged
to be married; she's just not sure who the groom will be. But now, at
least, she can rest. She went to the threshing floor with an empty future looming, and she has left with a promise. Her redeemer intends to
cover her, care for her, make her his bride.

We can't help but feel a sense of romance in this story, though that
may actually be reading too much into it. There's no explicit indication
that Boaz and Ruth have fallen in love. Ruth's primary concern is her un-
selfish desire to provide Naomi with an heir, not a selfish desire to find
herself a husband. Perhaps Boaz was already married and had children,
or maybe he was a widower. Or maybe he had never married and did, in
fact, find true love with Ruth late in his life. Whatever the case, Boaz was
determined to address the situation appropriately. Though everyone
around him was doing what was right in their own eyes, Boaz wanted
to do what was right in God's eyes in regard to the rights of redemption.

So Boaz went to the gate of the city where legal issues were handled.
And once again we witness a seeming coincidence, which, of course, is
no coincidence. The writer of Ruth tells us, "And behold, the redeemer,
of whom Boaz had spoken, came by" (Ruth 4:1). Don't miss the clever
way Boaz presents the opportunity at hand to the unnamed potential
redeemer. First, he presents the possibility of the purchase of the parcel
of land that belonged to Elimelech from Naomi. And immediately the
man says, yes, he will redeem it. But then Boaz completes the picture
of what the purchase will require.

> Then Boaz said, "The day you buy the field from the hand of Naomi, you
> also acquire Ruth the Moabite, the widow of the dead, in order to perpetu-
> ate the name of the dead in his inheritance." (Ruth 4:5)

Wait a minute. Now the deal doesn't look so good. If the man marries this young widow and she has a child, that child will inherit the land, and he will have just lost all the money he paid for it, money that would otherwise go to his own heirs. He would be spending his money to give a lasting name and inheritance to Elimelech, not to himself. So the deal is off. But Boaz is willing to pay the price. He will redeem.

> So Boaz took Ruth, and she became his wife. And he went in to her, and the
> LORD gave her conception, and she bore a son. (Ruth 4:13)

Ahhh. A satisfying conclusion to the story, so it seems. But, in fact, this is nowhere near the conclusion of the story.

> Boaz fathered Obed, Obed fathered Jesse, and Jesse fathered David.
> (Ruth 4:21–22)

Let's go back to our satellite lens. If we were to take another picture of these same fields outside Bethlehem a couple of generations after Ruth, we would see a young shepherd boy, strumming on his lyre, practicing with his sling-shot, caring for his father's flocks. He has a ruddy complexion and beautiful eyes and is quite handsome. And he doesn't know it yet, but someone is on the way to get him because Samuel has come to anoint him as the next king over Israel.

And if we were to take another picture of those same fields outside Bethlehem a thousand years later, we would find:

> There were shepherds out in the field, keeping watch over their flock by
> night. And an angel of the Lord appeared to them, and the glory of the Lord
> shone around them, and they were filled with great fear. And the angel
> said to them, "Fear not, for behold, I bring you good news of great joy that
> will be for all the people. For unto you is born this day in the city of David
> a Savior, who is Christ the Lord. (Luke 2:8–11)

Once again, the fields outside of Bethlehem were flooded with grace and with glory. Born in Bethlehem on that night was the true Redeemer that Boaz had shown God's people in shadow form. In Boaz's day, God had visited Bethlehem so that the people would not die of hunger. And once again, God visited Bethlehem so that his people will not die of hunger. On that starry night, God visited his people to give them the Bread of Life, the one who said, "Whoever comes to me shall not hunger" (John 6:35); the one about whom John wrote: "From his fullness we have all received, grace upon grace" (John 1:16).

⁓ Like Boaz, who was qualified to redeem because he was a close relative, Jesus was qualified to redeem by being "made like his brothers in every respect" (Heb. 2:17).

⁓ Like Boaz, who wanted Ruth to take refuge underneath his sheltering wings, Jesus said, "O Jerusalem, Jerusalem . . . how often would I have gathered your children together as a hen gathers her brood under her wings, and you were not willing!" (Luke 13:34).

⁓ Like Boaz, who spread the corner of his garment over Ruth, who had put herself at his feet, Christ spreads his robe of righteousness over anyone who will put herself or himself at his feet and ask for that covering.

⁓ Like Boaz, who rose from the threshing floor determined to go outside the gates of the city to do all that was legally necessary to redeem, Jesus determined to go outside the gates of the city and all the way to the cross to do all that was legally necessary to redeem, declaring when the work was done and the price was paid, "It is finished" (John 19:30).

Like Ruth, we were foreigners to God's grace, and we've been welcomed in by our Redeemer.

> Remember that you were at that time separated from Christ, alienated from the commonwealth of Israel and strangers to the covenants of promise, having no hope and without God in the world. *But now* in Christ Jesus you who once were far off have been brought near by the blood of Christ. . . . So then you are no longer strangers and aliens, but you are fellow citizens with the saints and members of the household of God. (Eph. 2:12–13, 19)

As the penniless foreigner Ruth cast herself at Boaz's feet, so we, alienated from God, unworthy and needy, cast ourselves at the feet of

Jesus. As she was dependent on the kindness and mercy of Boaz, so we have no hope other than the mercy of God. We need to be brought under the covering of the one who can provide peace and security. We need a bridegroom with integrity who will take us to himself.

Come and put yourself at the feet of the only one worthy to redeem you and say, "Fill up my emptiness. Take away my hunger. Take me from foreigner to family. Cover me. Give me a future. Make me into your pure bride. I come as one who has no provision, no protection, and I'm asking you to give me all these privileges out of the riches of your grace." He will overwhelm you with his kindness; he will fill your emptiness with his abundance; he will cover you with the robe of his righteousness. He will say to you, as Boaz said to Ruth, "And now, my daughter, do not fear. I will do for you all that you ask. As the Lord lives, I will redeem you."

Looking Forward

An Inheritance That Can't Be Lost, a Name That Can't Be Blotted Out

Part of what made Israel unique among the nations was that every family had its own inheritance of land. Land in Israel was meant to stay in the family as a reminder that God had provided and insured their inheritance. Each generation pushed the original inheritance into the future and assured the continuation of God's promise to all heirs, even those who had died. To die without an heir would mean that a family's inheritance of land in the Land of Promise would be lost along with God's promise to be his God and the God of his children. So it was a catastrophe when a man died without an heir.

Likewise, as is obvious partly from the emphasis on genealogies in the Old and New Testaments, having a name that endured through one's descendants was a vital part of being a partaker in the promises of God. To have a name that endures was to be connected to the life of God, and to have a name that perishes was to be cut off from God, which is why the psalmist praised God, saying, "You have made the wicked perish; you have blotted out their name forever and ever." To be blotted out from Israel was to be disconnected from God's people, God's land, and even God himself. So it was a catastrophe when a man died without an heir. How would the name of a man who died without an heir endure and not be blotted out?

In grace, God provided a way for this dilemma to be addressed. According to Deuteronomy 25:6, the first son born of a levirate union would "carry on the name of the dead brother so that his name will not be blotted out from Israel." A close relative could marry the widow for the purpose of producing an heir to inherit the land that belonged to the dead husband.

Thus, Boaz was a redeemer in two senses. When Boaz married Ruth and had a son, that firstborn son was considered a son of Elimelech, not of Boaz. Boaz said, "Ruth the Moabite, the widow of Mahlon, I have bought to be my wife, to perpetuate the name of the dead in his inheritance, *that the name of the dead may not be cut off from among his brothers and from the gate of his native place*" (Ruth 4:10). Second, when Boaz redeemed the parcel of land sold by Naomi, it didn't become his but was restored to Elimelech's line. In this way, Elimelech did not lose his inheritance in the Promised Land.

Likewise, our Redeemer has done all that is necessary so that we will inherit the land God has promised, and our names will not be blotted out. Because he has redeemed us, we can rest knowing that he will cover us, he will care for us, he will claim us as his bride. He promises, "The one who conquers will be clothed thus in white garments, and I will never blot his name out of the book of life. I will confess his name before my Father and before his angels" (Rev. 3:5).

Because of our sin, our name should perish with us. But because we have been redeemed, our name will not perish but will endure into eternity. We have no merit to make a claim to an inheritance in God's promised land—the new heaven and the new earth. But our Redeemer has paid the necessary price. He will one day welcome us into his land, granting to us our inheritance, where we will live forever with him.

Discussion Guide

Ruth

Getting the Discussion Going

1. Try to put yourself in the sandals of Naomi as she comes back into Bethlehem after being gone for ten years, and people hardly recognize her because of the toll her losses have taken. She doesn't want them to call her by her name, which means "sweetness." Instead, she wants them to call her a name that reflects the circumstances of her life and the state of her heart: bitter. What do you think about Naomi's bitterness? Can you relate to it? Is it justified? What assumptions about life and God have left her so bitter?

Getting to the Heart of It

2. Two themes that run throughout the book of Ruth are those of emptiness and fullness. Where do you see them in these four chapters, and what do you think the author of the book was trying to communicate through these themes?

3. In the Gospels we find these same themes of emptiness and fullness. John writes of the redeemer Jesus: "From his fullness we have all received, grace upon grace" (John 1:16). What examples can you think of in the Gospels of Jesus filling what was empty? (You'll find some hints, if needed, in Luke 5:4–6 and in John 2:6–11; 6:12; and 21:8.)

4. A key word in this book is *favor*, which is the Old Testament word for "grace." Since we recognize that Boaz is a type or shadow of Christ in this story, what does the favor Boaz showed to Ruth reveal to us about the favor or grace Christ shows to those who come to him asking to be redeemed?

5. Someone read aloud Ephesians 2:11–22. What key words or phrases jump out to you that describe Ruth and her experience? How does her experience help us to understand what our lives are like outside of Christ and what it means to be united to him?

6. Boaz said to Ruth, "The LORD repay you for what you have done, and a full reward be given you by the LORD, the God of Israel, under whose wings you have come to take refuge!" Jesus said, "Everyone who has left houses or brothers or sisters or father or mother or children or lands, for my name's sake, will receive a hundredfold and will inherit eternal life" (Matt. 19:29). How were Boaz's prayer and Jesus's promise borne out in Ruth's experience?

Getting Personal

7. The women around Naomi in Bethlehem told her that having Ruth as a daughter-in-law was better than having seven sons. "Seven sons" was another way of saying, "the perfect family." So they said to Naomi that what God was doing in her life through emptying her of her plans for her perfect family and perfect life was better than she could have ever put together for herself. God was doing something in her family that was much bigger than just redeeming her little family. Through her family would come not only the great King David but also the King of kings, the great Redeemer who offers redemption to all the families of the earth. Few of us have what we could call "the perfect family." Have you struggled with bitterness or disappointment in regard to your less-than-perfect family as Naomi did? Can you see ways that God is doing something good in your life or the lives of others through your less-than-perfect family? What would it mean for your sense of disappointment if you were to take hold of this hope?

Getting How It Fits into the Big Picture

8. God's promise to Abraham was that through him all the nations of the earth would be blessed. How would this story of Ruth have informed Old Testament believers about how that was going to happen and what role a greater redeemer would play?

1 Samuel

Personal Bible Study
1 Samuel

1. In the book of Judges we read that there was no king in Israel. And the book of Ruth was all about God preserving a faithful remnant in idolatrous Israel, from whom a king would one day come. How do the following verses add to the expectation that there will be a king over Israel?

Genesis 17:6:

Genesis 49:10:

Deuteronomy 17:14–20:

After having a series of judges who ruled over various segments of Israel for brief periods of crisis, God raised up the final judge, Samuel. Samuel ruled over Israel for many years, calling them back to the Lord, and speaking God's Word to them as a prophet, and offering sacrifices on their behalf as a priest.

2. Read 1 Samuel 8:1–22. What two motivations do the Israelites have for wanting a king?

3. This request feels to Samuel like a rejection of his leadership, but what does the Lord say it really is?

4. Read 1 Samuel 10:17–27. What about Saul made an impression on the people when they found him hiding with the baggage?

5. 1 Samuel 10:25 says that Samuel told the people the rights and duties of kingship and wrote them in a book. These rights and duties are found in Deuteronomy 17:14–20, a passage we read earlier. Summarize the rights and duties you find in each of the following verses:

v. 15

v. 15

v. 16

v. 17

v. 18

v. 19

6. Read 1 Samuel 13:1–14 and describe in two or three sentences what Saul did and the consequences of his actions.

7. Read 1 Samuel 16:1–13. How was Eliab similar to Saul?

8. What impression do we get about David from these verses?

9. Read 1 Samuel 17. The Israelites had wanted a king who would go out into battle for them. How is that working out for them?

10. What is at stake in this battle, according to Goliath's proposal in verses 8 and 9?

11. According to verse 26, what bothers David about Goliath's challenge?

12. On what basis was David confident that he could defeat Goliath?

13. David went out confident in his God, and Goliath cursed David by his gods (v. 43). What does this reveal about the true meaning of this battle?

14. In fact, this is really just another battle in the war between the offspring of the woman and the offspring of the Serpent that has been raging since Eden. Trace this battle and its participants and tactics throughout the Bible by identifying the enemy, the champion, and the method of victory in each of the following passages:

	Gen. 3:15	1 Samuel 17	Heb. 2:14; 12:2	Rom. 16:20; Rev. 12:9–11
The defeated enemy of God				
The victorious champion of God				
How the victory was accomplished				

15. When we begin to see this battle between David and Goliath as part of the greater battle that spans the history of redemption, we recognize that David reveals many things to us about his greater son, Jesus. Work

your way through the following statements about David from 1 Samuel 16 and 17 and write a corresponding statement about Jesus.

David	Jesus
David was born in Bethlehem. (1 Sam. 16:4)	Matt. 2:1
David was a shepherd. (1 Sam. 16:11)	John 10:11
David did not seem to be great—even to his own family. (1 Sam. 16:11)	Matt. 13:55–56; John 1:46
David was anointed among his brothers, and the Spirit of the Lord rushed upon him. (1 Sam. 16:13)	Matt. 3:16; Acts 10:38
David was sent by his father to his brothers. (1 Sam. 17:17)	John 8:42

David	Jesus
David was rejected and mocked and accused by his brothers of having evil motives. (1 Sam. 17:28)	John 1:11; Matt. 27:12, 41–42
David was confident of God's victory as he faced Goliath. (1 Sam. 17:37)	Matt. 20:17–19
David went out to face Goliath alone but with the presence of God. (1 Sam. 17:40, 45)	John 16:32
The sword that Goliath intended to use to slay David was used to destroy Goliath. (1 Sam. 17:50–51)	Col. 2:15
By destroying Goliath, David delivered the Israelites from being subject to lifelong slavery to the Philistines. (1 Sam. 17:9, 52)	Heb. 2:14–15
All of Israel shared in the victory over the Philistines, achieved by David as their representative. (1 Sam. 17:52)	1 Cor. 15:55–57

Teaching Chapter

We Won

I might as well admit it up front: I'm not a big sports fan. I've got nothing against sports, mind you, I just have a hard time working up much fervor in regard to who wins the big game or pretty much any game. Of course this puts me in the minority, not only in my own household where sports prognostications, statistics, and assessments are standard conversational fare, but also, it would seem, in the whole of humanity.

If you are a sports fan, or if you are ever around sports fans, then at one time or another you will have heard those fans say, "We won!" Now, this is interesting, because these fans are people who did not practice for the game, did not suit up for the game, and, in fact, were nowhere near the playing field. Most of them were not even on the sidelines or in the stands. And yet they can say with a straight face, "*We* won!" Somewhere along the way they have merged their identity, their aspirations, and their destiny with that of the team. Die-hard fans see the players who march onto the field or onto the court as extensions of themselves. They are joined to those brave warriors by common colors, if not shared effort, and by their passion for victory instead of defeat.

This story is actually about the most significant battle in the universe, a conflict in which the entire human race is at stake.

The history books of the Old Testament that we've been studying have more to do with battlefields than with playing fields, but there are some similarities. In the scene we witness today, a lone warrior goes out to battle while everyone else stays on the sidelines. And yet when the battle is over, all of those who have merged their identity and destiny with the victor could rightly shout and say, "We won!" even though they were never on the field. But, of course, this isn't a game. In fact, when we look closely, we'll discover that this story is actually about the most significant battle in the universe, a conflict in which the entire human race is at stake.

Anticipated King

We began our study in Joshua, and since then life in Israel has gone from the heights of entering and possessing the land to the depths of utter chaos and catastrophe. The writer of Judges stated the problem clearly: there was no king in Israel. And when we came to the end of the story of Ruth, the writer seemed to be pointing us toward the solution to that problem, a descendant of Boaz and Ruth who will become the great king of Israel. And as we open up 1 Samuel, we find a barren woman named Hannah. She has come to the house of the Lord at Shiloh, and she is pouring out her brokenhearted, desperate prayer to the Lord, promising that if he will give her a child, she will give that child back to him. A few years later she is back in Shiloh with the young son God gave to her. She is following through on her commitment, bringing Samuel to live out his days with the priests. One would think that her heart would be heavy, and surely there were tears in her eyes, but her mouth was full of song. And in the closing words of her prayer, we sense that Hannah has seen beyond herself and her son when she says:

> The LORD will judge the ends of the earth;
>   He will give strength to his king
>   and exalt the power of his anointed. (1 Sam. 2:10)

When she prayed this prayer, there was no king in Israel, and yet she prayed that God will give strength to his king. More than that, she has seen that this king will be the Lord's anointed. Hannah's prayer is really a prophecy. Hannah is able to see past the Lord's work in her little life into the expanse of the whole world, and beyond the years of her life into the distant future. The Hebrew word for "anointed" is *messiah* and translated into Greek it becomes *Christos*, or Christ. Hannah's heart is celebrating not only God's work in her own womb but God's work in the womb of another ordinary Israelite who will one day give birth to the king God has always intended to rule over his earth, the Messiah King.

Rejected King

Hannah's son, Samuel, grew up serving the priests and eventually became a great prophet and judge of Israel. He called the people back to the Lord and prayed to the Lord for the people. But Samuel grew old, and his sons were unfit to take his place. That's when the people of Israel came to Samuel with a proposal.

> "Behold, you are old and your sons do not walk in your ways. Now appoint for us a king to judge us like all the nations." But the thing displeased Samuel when they said, "Give us a king to judge us." (1 Sam. 8:5–6)

The problem with their proposal was not that they wanted a king. The problem was that they'd forgotten that they already had a king! Their warrior King had destroyed the Egyptian army and brought down the walls of Jericho and defeated many other foes without the Israelites' even raising a sword. If they would submit single-heartedly to the king they had—God himself—they would never experience defeat in battle. But they no longer saw their battles as the Lord's battles, and they wanted the security that they thought a human king with his standing army could provide. Instead of returning to their King in glad submission, they rejected their King in naive rebellion.

A second problem with their proposal was the kind of king they wanted. They wanted a king like other nations had so that they could "be like all the nations" (1 Sam. 8:20). God had brought them out of Egypt to be a kingdom of priests, a blessing to other nations by being distinct from them, but they didn't want to be set apart; they wanted to fit in. They wanted to operate like the other nations who trusted in the military might and savvy of a king they could see instead of trusting a divine king they could not see. Even though God had always promised to go out before them in battle, they said they wanted a human king to "go out before us and fight our battles" (1 Sam. 8:20).

Obviously God had always intended that one day there would be a kingship in Israel. When God made his covenant with Abraham, he told him that kings would come from him (Gen. 17:6). When Jacob gave his final blessing to his sons, he prophesied of a kingship that would come from the tribe of Judah and rule over Israel (Gen. 49:10). Back in the book of Deuteronomy, God gave a profile of the person who should be king among his people. It wasn't that this desire for a king was evil; the problem was that they wanted "the wrong king, for all the wrong reasons, at the wrong time, and from the wrong initiation."[1]

> And Samuel prayed to the LORD. And the LORD said to Samuel, "Obey the voice of the people in all that they say to you, for they have not rejected you, but they have rejected me from being king over them." (1 Sam. 8:6–7)

Oftentimes in the Bible we see that God judges people not by withholding what they ask for but by giving them what they ask for. The Hebrew word for *Saul* is a form of the verb "to ask," and when God gave them Saul, he seemed to be just what the people were asking for. He was tall and handsome and looked the part. The Lord told Samuel:

> You shall anoint him to be prince over my people Israel. He shall save my people from the hand of the Philistines. For I have seen my people, because their cry has come to me. (1 Sam. 9:16)

He has heard their cry and given them a leader, but notice that God says to anoint a prince over his people, not a king. Rather than reigning as an absolute monarch, whoever is king over Israel will be subject to God's word mediated through his prophet.

Because Israel was God's people and the Philistines were the enemies of God, confronting those enemies was supposed to be more like a worship service than like a war. Preparation for battle was more about offering sacrifices than sharpening swords. Preparations sounded more like hearing God's word from God's spokesman, the prophet, than hear-

---

[1] Michael D. Williams, *Far as the Curse Is Found: The Covenant Story of Redemption* (Phillipsburg, NJ: P&R, 2005), 180.

ing military strategists giving orders. Samuel told Saul to wait for him in Gilgal, where he would offer sacrifice on Israel's behalf before engaging the Philistines. But while Saul was waiting for Samuel to arrive, his soldiers were slipping away and going home. Saul decided he just couldn't wait for the prophet to give him the instructive word of the Lord. So he assumed the role of priest and offered sacrifices himself and prepared for battle. Right then Samuel finally showed up, and Saul felt caught. Saul said to Samuel:

> "I forced myself, and offered the burnt offering." And Samuel said to Saul, "You have done foolishly. You have not kept the command of the LORD your God, with which he commanded you. For then the LORD would have established your kingdom over Israel forever. But now your kingdom shall not continue. The LORD has sought out a man after his own heart, and the LORD has commanded him to be prince over his people, because you have not kept what the LORD commanded you." (1 Sam. 13:12–14)

Here we find the expression that we usually hear as "a man after God's own heart," which makes us picture a man who has a heart *like* God's heart or a man who is pursuing knowing the heart of God. But the expression is literally "the Lord has sought for himself a man according to his own heart."[2] Samuel is saying that God is looking for a king to sit on the throne over Israel who suits his desires and purposes rather than the kind of king that suits the people's desires and purposes. In Saul, God had given the people the kind of king *they* wanted. But now the Lord was about to give the people the kind of king *he* wanted.

The people had rejected God as their king, and now God has rejected Saul as the people's king. Saul had shown "a fundamental inability or unwillingness to submit to the divine rule as mediated through the prophet, and therefore a fundamental unsuitability to be king in Israel."[3]

> The LORD said to Samuel, "How long will you grieve over Saul, since I have rejected him from being king over Israel? Fill your horn with oil, and go.

---

[2]John Woodhouse, *1 Samuel: Looking for a Leader*, Preaching the Word, ed. R. Kent Hughes (Wheaton, IL: Crossway, 2008), 235.
[3]Iain William Provan, V. Philips Long, and Tremper Longman, *A Biblical History of Israel* (Louisville: Westminster, 2003), 214.

I will send you to Jesse the Bethlehemite, for I have provided for myself a king among his sons." (1 Sam. 16:1)

When Samuel saw Jesse and his sons, Samuel was sure he saw Saul's replacement. David's older brother, Eliab, tall and handsome, looked kingly just as Saul had looked like a king.

But the LORD said to Samuel, "Do not look on his appearance or on the height of his stature, because I have rejected him. For the LORD sees not as man sees: man looks on the outward appearance, but the LORD looks on the heart." (1 Sam. 16:7)

Then Samuel said to Jesse, "Are all your sons here?" And he said, "There remains yet the youngest, but behold, he is keeping the sheep." (1 Sam. 16:11)

Unexpected King

Evidently David was so insignificant to the family that he wasn't even called in from the fields to be included in this once-in-a-lifetime honor of offering a sacrifice with Israel's great judge, Samuel. But that was about to change.

And he sent and brought him in. Now he was ruddy and had beautiful eyes and was handsome. (1 Sam. 16:12)

David was handsome but hardly impressive. He knew how to handle sheep, but there was no sign that he knew how to handle a nation. He had proven himself in the grazing fields but was unproven on the battlefield. Yet this was the unlikely king God had chosen. Samuel could see only the outward appearance, which evidently did not appear very royal. But God could see into David's heart. David may not have been impressive, but he had integrity. He may not have had proven battle skills, but he did have a passion for God's honor. This is what God was looking for in a king over Israel.

Do you find it a comforting thing or a condemning thing to consider that God sees and knows the heart? God sees through our reputations into the reality for good and for bad. Some of us look so good on the outside, and no one would guess what is really going on inside our hearts. People around us can't always see the stubborn disobedience, the steady stream of defeats in our battles against ongoing sin, the stifling darkness that defines the real culture of our inner lives. But God does. Likewise, other people can't always see the secret sacrifices, the costly surrenders, all the little deaths to self that define the culture of hearts that have been invaded by and are ruled by King Jesus. But God does.

Anointed King

Everyone in Jesse's house must have been surprised and perhaps even confused when:

> Samuel took the horn of oil and anointed [David] in the midst of his brothers. (1 Sam. 16:13)

Throughout the Old Testament, people were consecrated for divine service, such as priesthood and kingship, through an anointing ceremony. As the oil dripped down the face and beard, it was a visual representation of God pouring out his Spirit on the man, empowering him for his holy duties. To be anointed was to be set aside and equipped by God and for God. A person anointed by God acted in God's name with the help of God's Spirit, under God's protection, and with God's authority.

> And the Spirit of the LORD rushed upon David from that day forward.
> (1 Sam. 16:13)

Up to this point in the Old Testament scriptures, we have read about the Spirit of the Lord rushing upon people chosen by God for various tasks to empower them for those tasks. But this was different. In the other cases, the "rushing upon" of the Spirit was temporary. But this was "from that day forward." It was permanent. All of Israel's history had been pointing toward that day and the anointing of this shepherd king. David had become the Lord's anointed, the Christ. We can't help but see in David's life the shadows of the Lord's anointed, the Messiah, Christ Jesus, cast backward into history. And once we begin to see David in this light, it begins to change everything about the way we've always understood what happens next.

Embattled King

The people had originally asked for a king because of the threat from the Philistines, so it does not surprise us to read at the beginning of chapter 17:

> Now the Philistines gathered their armies for battle. (1 Sam. 17:1)

The Philistines who were gathered at Socoh—uncomfortably close to the heart of Israel—were not just another enemy. They were a threat to Israel's existence. Saul had had mixed results in his previous jousts with them, and this time there was a new wrinkle in the conflict:

> And there came out from the camp of the Philistines a champion named Goliath of Gath, whose height was six cubits and a span. (1 Sam. 17:4)

Goliath, this Philistine among Philistines, was 9 feet tall. But he wasn't just tall; he seemed to have superhuman strength.

> He had a helmet of bronze on his head, and he was armed with a coat of mail, and the weight of the coat was five thousand shekels of bronze. And he had bronze armor on his legs, and a javelin of bronze slung between his shoulders. The shaft of his spear was like a weaver's beam, and his spear's head weighed six hundred shekels of iron. And his shield-bearer went before him. (1 Sam. 17:5–7)

Goliath was covered head to toe with the high-tech weaponry of his day—bronze. This bronze armor was heavy; it weighed 125 pounds. He carried a spear with a tip that weighed 15 pounds, so it was like he had a 15-pound bowling ball on the end of his spear, and it was seemingly nothing to him to carry and project this heavy spear through the air toward his adversaries. But what is a "coat of mail"? Other translations call it a coat of "scale armor." His bronze armor was like the scales of a snake. Picture this: when Goliath went out onto the battlefield he was covered in what looked like snakeskin from head to toe. He's like a 9-foot-tall serpent.[4] And he has an alternative proposal to bloody battle between the two armies. So he shouted to all of the ranks of Israel:

> Choose a man for yourselves, and let him come down to me. If he is able to fight with me and kill me, then we will be your servants. But if I prevail against him and kill him, then you shall be our servants and serve us. (1 Sam. 17:8–9)

Goliath has challenged them to "choose a man" to go out before them in battle, and of course, Israel *had* chosen a man for this. That had been the whole point of demanding a king. They had told Samuel that they wanted a king who would "go out before us and fight our battles" (1 Sam. 8:19–20). But Saul, the tallest man among the Israelites, the most likely man to go out and face this giant, is back hiding in his tent, just as scared as the rest of them. For forty days straight, Goliath has come out and issued the same challenge, and seemingly Saul has no intentions of going out to meet him.

Goliath is undiluted evil. If the person who goes out to battle for Israel loses this battle, all Israel will be in bondage to this evil. It would seem that all Israel was destined to become slaves of the Philistines—until hope showed up. Verse 12 begins, "Now David . . ." The shepherd boy had been sent to the battlefront with food for his brothers. When he got there and heard the threats of Goliath, he could hardly believe it. This goon from Gath was insulting the God of Israel, and no one among the Israelites seemed to care. No one else in the camp seemed a bit offended for God's honor. But David was. And so he asked:

> Who is this uncircumcised Philistine, that he should defy the armies of the living God? (1 Sam. 17:26)

The Israelite army saw Goliath as unbeatable, but David saw him as uncircumcised—wholly without the presence and power and promises of God.[5] David understood that to taunt and mock and threaten the people of God is to taunt and mock and threaten God himself. He sim-

---

[4] I learned this astonishing and significant connection between Goliath's armor and the great Serpent in listening to Liam Goligher's sermon "Giant Killer" (Duke Street Church, London, November 13, 2011).
[5] This contrast between the way the Israelite army saw Goliath and the way David saw him comes from Alistair Begg's sermon "Seeing What David Saw" (Parkside Church, Chagrin Falls, Ohio, October 24, 2004).

ply couldn't understand how anyone could stand for it, so he offered himself to Saul.

> Let no man's heart fail because of him. Your servant will go and fight with this Philistine. (1 Sam. 17:32)

David, with one smooth stone hurled at Goliath, crushed the head of the serpent.

Before David could battle against Goliath, he had to do battle with the derision of his brother Eliab, who simply wanted his little brother to be quiet and go away. David also had to do battle with Saul's belittling. Saul was understandably concerned about the tremendous size and experience differential between Goliath and David. But David was not focused on his adversary's size or experience. He was resting in his own experience of God's deliverance in lesser battles against lions and bears and in Yahweh's covenant promise to save his people.

> Then he took his staff in his hand and chose five smooth stones from the brook and put them in his shepherd's pouch. His sling was in his hand, and he approached the Philistine. (1 Sam. 17:40)

So David went out to fight Goliath. The weight of the future of God's people rested on this shepherd boy. David, however, was confident— not in himself but in God's conquering power. And though he was insulted by Goliath, he wasn't intimidated by him.

> Then David said to the Philistine, "You come to me with a sword and with a spear and with a javelin, but I come to you in the name of the Lord of hosts, the God of the armies of Israel, whom you have defied. This day the Lord will deliver you into my hand, and I will strike you down and cut off your head." (1 Sam. 17:45–46)

Goliath has blasphemed the God of Israel. And under the law of Israel, what is to be done to blasphemers? They are to be stoned (Lev. 24:16). David, the Lord's anointed, was about to become "the Lord's instrument to bring about the Lord's vengeance on the Lord's enemy for the Lord's glory.[6] David, with one smooth stone hurled at Goliath, crushed the head of the serpent.

> So David prevailed over the Philistine with a sling and with a stone, and struck the Philistine and killed him. There was no sword in the hand of David. Then David ran and stood over the Philistine and took his sword and drew it out of its sheath and killed him and cut off his head with it. When the Philistines saw that their champion was dead, they fled. (1 Sam. 17:50–51)

Victorious King

David, the Lord's anointed, was victorious. The Israelites would not have to become the slaves of the Philistines. The victory won single-handedly by the Lord's anointed became the shared victory of God's people. They didn't go out to battle, yet they could claim victory vicariously through the one who represented them on the field of battle. And as the reality of this sinks in, as the greater battle between the Lord's anointed and the Lord's enemy comes into focus, can you see that we too are being swept into this victory?

Oftentimes, when we heard this story taught in Sunday school, or when we've taught the story in Sunday school, this is the point in the story when the challenge is given to be like David—to have David's faith and confidence in God, to have his courage in fighting the giants in our lives, and to trust God to make us victorious over whatever difficulties we face. In that version, the lesson to be learned from David and Goliath is that it's up to us to step up to the plate and have faith like David so that God can give us the kind of victory that David had over Goliath. But, in reality, we are not meant to see ourselves in David's place in this story. Instead, we are to see ourselves back there in the ranks of Israel's army, shaking and afraid, intimidated and tired. Our efforts at finding someone to rule on the throne of our lives who will be our champion and protector have completely failed, and it looks like we will be slaves forever to our greatest enemy, Satan himself.

But we have a champion. It's a boy from Bethlehem. He did not look

---

[6]Goligher, "Giant Killer."

strong or kingly but more like a shepherd. He was sent to us by our Father, and we rejected him and mocked him and just wanted to silence him. He refused to arm himself with the kind of armor that everyone knows is needed to get ahead in this world—the kind that impresses and intimidates and overpowers. He wasn't concerned with preserving his own safety but only with preserving God's honor. And when he went into battle against the great enemy of his people, he went alone. There, not in the valley of Elah but on the hill of Calvary, our champion was victorious—not through impressive strength but in crushing weakness. There, on the cross, Jesus, the offspring of the woman, experienced the bruising of his heel. There, our champion crushed the head of the ancient Serpent.

> That through death he might destroy the one who has the power of death, that is, the devil, and deliver all those who through fear of death were subject to lifelong slavery. (Heb. 2:14–15)

If the Goliath of death had defeated Jesus, we would forever be slaves to death. But our champion defeated death by his resurrection. His victory over death has become our victory over death, so we can mock it as hollow threats:

> "O death, where is your victory?
>   O death, where is your sting?"

> The sting of death is sin, and the power of sin is the law. But thanks be to God, who gives us the victory through our Lord Jesus Christ. (1 Cor. 15:55–57)

Like David, *Jesus was an anticipated king.* Hannah's heart sang, "My heart exults in the LORD," when it was revealed to her that God was going to miraculously give her a child and would one day put a king on the throne. So Mary's heart also sang, "My soul magnifies the Lord," when the angel told her that she would miraculously have a son who would be that king over the entire earth.

Jesus was a rejected king. The people of Jesus's day were looking for a king like the kings of the nations around them, a king who would exercise military might and save them from human oppressors. And when Pilate presented him to the Jews, saying, "Behold your King!" they made it clear that he was not the kind of king they wanted, crying out, "Away with him, crucify him!" (John 19:14–15). Jesus, the Lord's anointed, was rejected by those he came to save.

Like David, *Jesus was an unexpected king.* Jesus didn't have an outward appearance that would lead anyone to recognize him as a king. The prophet Isaiah described him as having "no form or majesty that we should look

> *Our champion was victorious—not through impressive strength but in crushing weakness.*

at him, and no beauty that we should desire him" (Isa. 53:2). He ruled over his people in an unexpected way, saying, "You know that the rulers of the Gentiles lord it over them, and their great ones exercise authority over them. . . . The Son of Man came not to be served but to serve" (Matt. 20:25–28).

Like David, *Jesus was an anointed king.* He was set apart by the Spirit from his very conception. The angel told Mary, "The Holy Spirit will come upon you, and the power of the Most High will overshadow you; therefore the child to be born will be called holy—the Son of God" (Luke 1:35). He was publicly anointed at his baptism when "the heavens were opened, and the Holy Spirit descended on him in bodily form, like a dove" (Luke 3:21–22). His third anointing came when he ascended into heaven to sit at the right hand of God. The writer to the Hebrews uses the words of the psalmist to celebrate this anointing, writing: "*But of the Son he says,* 'Your throne, O God, is forever and ever, the scepter of uprightness is the scepter of your kingdom. You have loved righteousness and hated wickedness; therefore God, your God, has anointed you with the oil of gladness beyond your companions'" (Heb. 1:8–9).

And, finally, like David, *Jesus is a victorious king.* We face an enemy, an army of enemies in fact, who are as real, as powerful, and as terrifying as Goliath. "For we do not wrestle against flesh and blood, but against the rulers, against the authorities, against the cosmic powers over this present darkness, against the spiritual forces of evil in the heavenly places" (Eph. 6:12). Our enemy is not covered in bronze and hurling heavy spears. He is armed with darkness and deception. He hurls condemnation at us and lies to us and inflicts us with pleasures that only bring pain. He threatens to enslave us to destructive addictions and defeating patterns and incapacitating fears. And we would turn and run, certain that we are doomed—except that we have a champion. Just when we are tempted to give way to despair, we hear the voice of the Son of David saying, "Let no man's heart fail. Your servant will go and fight."

Jesus has defeated the enemy that threatened us with lifelong slavery to death. And if God is for us in Christ, who can be against us? Shall tribulation, or distress, or persecution, or famine, or nakedness, or danger, or sword? . . . No in all these things we are more than conquerors—not because we are strong, not because we can win the battle if we just have faith like David's—we are more than conquerors *through him* who loved us (Rom. 8:31–37). Our victory and security come from being united to our champion. Because our Shepherd Warrior King has gone out before us and has crushed the head of the Serpent, we can rightly say, "We won!" and know that we will share in his victory forever.

~~~~~~

Looking Forward

A Gruesome Feast

Goliath saw David as a little twig that would easily snap under his strength. He intended to make quick work of him and serve him up as supper for the birds.

> The Philistine said to David, "Come to me, and I will give your flesh to the birds of the air and to the beasts of the field." (1 Sam. 17:44)

But David had no intention of becoming bird food. Instead, he intended that Goliath and all of those who opposed the armies of the living God would be served up for supper:

> Then David said to the Philistine, "You come to me with a sword and with a spear and with a javelin, but I come to you in the name of the LORD of hosts, the God of the armies of Israel, whom you have defied. This day the LORD will deliver you into my hand, and I will strike you down and cut off your head. And I will give the dead bodies of the host of the Philistines this day to the birds of the air and to the wild beasts of the earth, that all the earth may know that there is a God in Israel." (1 Sam. 17:45–46)

After David cut off the head of Goliath, "the men of Israel and Judah rose with a shout and pursued the Philistines as far as Gath and the gates of Ekron, so that the wounded Philistines fell on the way from Shaaraim as far as Gath and Ekron" (1 Sam. 17:52). Sure enough, the fallen enemies of God lay strewn for miles, becoming a feast for the birds of the air and the beasts of the field. But evidently this was only a picture of a much greater feast for the birds to come. The Old Testament prophet Ezekiel later foretold of a coming judgment in which birds of prey will be invited to a feast to feed upon the flesh of those defeated by Israel's God:

> As for you, son of man, thus says the Lord GOD: Speak to the birds of every sort and to all beasts of the field, "Assemble and come, gather from all around to the sacrificial feast that I am preparing for you, a great sacrificial feast on the mountains of Israel, and you shall eat flesh and drink blood. You shall eat the flesh of the mighty, and drink the blood of the princes of the earth—of rams, of lambs, and of he-goats, of bulls, all of them fat beasts of Bashan. And you shall eat fat till you are filled, and drink blood till you are drunk, at the sacrificial feast that I am preparing for you. And you shall be filled at my table with horses and charioteers, with mighty men and all kinds of warriors," declares the Lord GOD. (Ezek. 39:17–20)

This is a gruesome scene that we would really rather not look at. But we must. Allowing ourselves to look at this scene instills us with urgency to warn all of those who have set themselves against God about what is to come if they continue in rebellion. And for God's people who live under the painful hand of persecution, this scene instills confidence that one day their suffering will end and God will set things right.

The apostle John was given a vision of the fulfillment of this gruesome feast prefigured on the fields of battle in David's time and prophesied by Ezekiel. Revelation 19 pulls back the curtain for us to see the gruesome feast that will be served up at the final battle between the Lord's anointed, the King of kings, and the enemies of God. The first half of Revelation 19 describes the great feast that all of those who belong to Christ will enjoy—the marriage supper of the Lamb (Rev. 19:7). But the joyous account of that feast is followed by an account of another feast at which there is no celebration.

> Then I saw an angel standing in the sun, and with a loud voice he called to all the birds that fly directly overhead, "Come, gather for the great supper of God, to eat the flesh of kings, the flesh of captains, the flesh of mighty men, the flesh of horses and their riders, and the flesh of all men, both free and slave, both small and great." (Rev. 19:16–18)

God himself also issues the invitation to this banquet, but it goes out to all the birds of prey. This will be a feast for the wild animals after the judgment of those who rebel against God. If you belong to Christ you have nothing to fear as you anticipate that day. All of those who are pledged to our great Bridegroom can look forward to the consummation of our marriage and being loved forever by the Lamb. But all of those who have rejected him and ignored him have nothing to look forward to and everything to dread.

Discussion Guide

1 Samuel

Getting the Discussion Going

1. Imagine that you were a witness to the scene day after day in the Valley of Elah as Goliath came out to taunt the Israelites with his offer to fight a single foe, and that you were there watching David walk out to face him. What do you think it sounded like? And how did it feel to be there? What might you have observed on both sides of the battle lines?

Getting to the Heart of It

2. Goliath came out every day for forty days challenging and taunting the Israelites. Our enemy mocks and taunts us every day, too. What are some things our enemy, the Devil, says to intimidate us? How can we experience victory in this daily battle?

3. Some of us have been taught this story all of our lives with a moral of something like, "If you will trust God, he will give you the courage to face whatever bad things come." But what difference does it make if we see ourselves in the place of Israel's army instead of as David in this story? How does that change what we are to take away from the story?

4. Through the narratives of 1 Samuel, there is a constant clash between worldly strength and godly strength, between worldly desires and godly desires. What are some of the contrasts you see between David and Saul and between David and Goliath in this regard?

5. Someone read aloud 1 Corinthians 1:22–29. How does this passage capture what happened with David and Goliath? And how does this passage both instruct and encourage you about being used by God to make a gospel impact in your world?

6. This story reminds us that as we take the word of Christ to an unbelieving world, we go to do battle. As modern Christians we tend to see ourselves as selling a product, not fighting a battle. We are marketers, not soldiers. We face potential customers, not an enemy. But the New Testament often describes what we are to be about in battle terms (Eph. 6:10–20). What difference does it make to understand that we are in a battle, a battle that is the Lord's battle?

7. Look back at the Personal Bible Study where you explored some of the ways David points to Christ. What were some that were especially interesting or meaningful to you?

8. Once we recognize that David, the Lord's anointed (which means "messiah" or "Christ"), is meant to point us toward Jesus, the Lord's anointed, we realize that Goliath is meant to point us toward the Lord's enemy, Satan. What are some of the ways we see Satan himself in Goliath?

Getting Personal

9. When you consider "the LORD sees not as man sees: man looks on the outward appearance, but the LORD looks on the heart" (1 Sam.16:7), do you find that comforting or discomforting? Why?

Getting How It Fits into the Big Picture

10. Perhaps we've always seen this story of David's battle with Goliath as its own little Bible story, but in this lesson we've discovered that it is actually part of a much larger story. What is this battle really about, and where do you see it surface throughout Scripture?

2 Samuel

Personal Bible Study

2 Samuel

In 1 Samuel we read about Samuel anointing David to be king over Israel and about David's emergence on the scene by slaying Goliath. But Saul is still king. The second half of 1 Samuel focuses on Saul's demise as king and his relentless pursuit to kill David, while David, who became a commander in Saul's army, refused to harm Saul or take the throne by his own power. Second Samuel covers the remainder of David's life. It begins with David hearing about the death of Saul and Jonathan (2 Samuel 1) and David being anointed king—but he is not yet king over all of Israel. In 2 Samuel 2 David is anointed king over just the powerful southern tribe of Judah and sets up his headquarters in Hebron, where he will rule for seven and a half years. Abner, the commander of Saul's army, makes Ish-bosheth, one of Saul's sons, king over the northern tribes of Israel. Then we read at the beginning of chapter 3, "There was a long war between the house of Saul and the house of David. And David grew stronger and stronger, while the house of Saul became weaker and weaker" (v. 1). The war ended when two of Ish-bosheth's own captains killed him (2 Samuel 4).

1. Read 2 Samuel 5:1–5. What three reasons did the people of the tribes of Israel give for wanting David to be their king?

    1.

2.

3.

2. Read 2 Samuel 5:6–12 along with Exodus 3:8 and Deuteronomy 7:1. What did David accomplish that God had intended since he first came to Moses and gave him instructions to bring his people out of Egypt?

3. What happened in this city previously, according to the following verses?

Genesis 14:18:

Genesis 22:2:

4. Jerusalem was to be not only the political capital and military head-quarters but also the center of Israel's worship of God. How does 2 Samuel 6 reveal that David intended to be not only lead warrior of Israel but also lead worshiper?

5. Read 2 Samuel 7:1–3. What is the problem, as David sees it?

6. Initially Nathan told David, "Go, do all that is in your heart, for the LORD is with you," perhaps relying only on instinct or common sense; but that night the word of the Lord came to him with a message to give to David. How would you summarize the intent of God's initial questions in 7:5–7?

7. Identify the key aspects of God's covenant with David in the following verses:

v. 8

v. 9

v. 10

v. 11

v. 12

v. 13

v. 14

v. 15

v. 16

8. There is a bit of a play on words here, as "house" is used to refer to three different things. Describe what is meant by "house" in each of these verses:

7:1

7:5

7:11

9. Oftentimes, to understand biblical prophecies and promises, we have to see them like a distant mountain range. From far away, we can't differentiate between different mountains. We can't see that some mountains are closer and some are farther away. They seem like one long mountain. But the closer we get, or the more we bring them into view through a telescope, the clearer we can see that some of the individual mountains are closer than others. That's what we see in God's covenant promise to David, found in 2 Samuel 7. Some aspects of his promise were fulfilled in David's lifetime and some in the years immediately following his lifetime, when Solomon and other descendants sat on this throne as king over Israel. But those were just initial or partial fulfillments. They served as a preview of how God would fulfill his promises to David in a much greater way to David's greater descendant. The promises that God made to David find greater fulfillment in David's greater son, Jesus, in both his first coming and in his second. Work your way through the various aspects of God's promise to David in the following chart and note from the references provided how each aspect of the

promise was fulfilled in David's day, in Solomon's day, in the days of Jesus's first coming, in his current heavenly reign, and/or when Jesus comes again.

Promise	Fulfillment
I will make for you a great name. (2 Sam. 7:9)	2 Sam. 5:10 Phil. 2:10
I will appoint a place for my people Israel and will plant them, so that they may dwell in their own place and be disturbed no more. And violent men shall afflict them no more, as formerly. (2 Sam. 7:10)	John 14:1–3 Rev. 21:1–14
I will give you rest from all your enemies. (2 Sam. 7:11)	2 Sam. 7:1 1 Kings 5:4 1 Cor. 15:23–28
The LORD will make you a house. (2 Sam. 7:11)	1 Kings 11:43 Heb. 3:6

Promise	Fulfillment
I will raise up your offspring after you, who shall come from your body, and I will establish his kingdom. (2 Sam. 7:12)	1 Kings 1:46 Acts 2:29–36
He shall build a house for my name. (2 Sam. 7:13)	1 Kings 8:15–20 John 2:19–22
I will be to him a father, and he shall be to me a son. (2 Sam. 7:14–15)	Ps. 2:6–7 Rom. 1:3–4
When he commits iniquity, I will discipline him with the rod of men, with the stripes of the sons of men. (2 Sam. 7:14–15)	1 Kings 11:9–14 Isa. 53:5
My steadfast love will not depart from him, as I took it from Saul. (2 Sam. 7:15)	2 Kings 8:19

Promise	Fulfillment
Your house and your kingdom shall be made sure forever before me. (2 Sam. 7:16)	Luke 1:33 1 Pet. 2:4–5
Your throne shall be established forever. (2 Sam. 7:16)	Rev. 4:1–11; 22:16

10. Just as the levitical priesthood anticipated the superior priesthood of Jesus, and just as Old Testament prophets anticipated Jesus, the prophet par excellence, so David and his throne anticipated the reign of the coming King, Jesus. Read each statement below about the reign and kingdom of King David and write a corresponding or contrasting statement in the second column in regard to the reign and kingdom of King Jesus.

David's Reign	Jesus's Reign
David was the shepherd of God's people and prince over them. (2 Sam. 5:2)	Matt. 2:6; John 10:14, 16
David sat on the throne as king in Jerusalem, the earthly city of God. (2 Sam. 5:6–7)	Rev. 21:1–7

David's Reign	Jesus's Reign
Sinners who touched the presence of God in the ark died. (2 Sam. 6:6–7)	Matt. 9:20–22; 1 John 1:1
God raised David up from shepherding to sit on the throne of Israel. (2 Sam. 7:8)	Acts 2:24–25
David's son sat on his throne.	Luke 22:30; Rev. 3:21

Teaching Chapter

Forever

I thought about buying up a bunch of stamps a while ago before the postal rates were set to increase, and I should have done it. The beauty of Forever stamps is that you buy them at the current rate for mailing a first-class letter and they are supposed to be good for mailing a first-class letter forever, no matter how much the price of a first-class stamp increases. But the truth is, I hardly ever mail first-class letters anymore. Most of my communication with people is via e-mail or telephone or cell phone, and I pay most of my bills online. And evidently I'm not alone. Reports are that the US Postal Service is on the brink of bankruptcy. And if that's the case, maybe their promise of "forever" is really not all that reliable.

Speaking of forever, we've all heard the famous line "A diamond is forever." But is it true? Evidently, for the last twenty-five years a team of scientists have been trying to find out. At a site in central Japan, scientists have been monitoring a huge underground water-filled tank, waiting patiently for signs that all matter eventually decays into sub-atomic dust. Evidently, most theorists believe it will show that protons—the building blocks of every atom—do not last forever but decay into other particles. That would mean nothing made from atoms—not even diamonds—lasts forever.[1]

The Bible, however, talks about some things that do last forever.

---

[1] Robert Matthews, "Diamonds Aren't Forever," *Focus*, January 17, 2008.

"The steadfast love of the Lord endures forever" (Psalm 136). Forever the Lord will love his own.

"His righteousness endures forever" (Ps. 111:3). Forever God will be doing what is right.

"The faithfulness of the LORD endures forever" (Ps. 117:2). Forever God will do what he has promised to do and be who has promised to be.

"The grass withers, the flower fades, but the word of our God will stand forever" (Isa. 40:8). Forever God's Word will have the power to accomplish what it intends. Forever it will prove true.

The apostle John wrote: "The world is passing away along with its desires, but whoever does the will of God abides forever" (1 John 2:17). Evidently God intends to share his "foreverness" with those who find their life under his loving rule now. Does this kind of forever sound good to you? Let's face it; most of us have had experiences that *felt like* forever that we don't particularly want to experience again. So before we buy into this forever being offered to us, we want to know what we can expect.

Over three thousand years ago, God put a king on the throne in his city to rule over his people as his representative. The king who sat on this throne was never supposed to be a king like other kings in this world who rule independently and often tyrannically. Unlike any other kingdom and any other throne, this kingdom and this throne were established to last forever. But what does that mean and why does it matter? Here in 2 Samuel, as we look at the king God put on the earthly throne over his people—the throne that was to be an earthy extension of his heavenly throne—we get a glimpse of the forever God intends to give to us. David was the king who was according to God's own heart, the kind of king God wanted to rule over his people. As we listen in on the promises God made to his king, we'll discover that these promises shape the forever that God is inviting us into.

The King's City

David was a teenager when the prophet Samuel anointed him to be king over Israel. Twenty-five years later David was still not ruling on the throne. Instead he had spent those years leading armies into battle and ducking from Saul's spears and living out in the wilderness and even in foreign countries. Second Samuel picks up the history of Israel immediately after Saul's death. In chapter 2 we read that David was finally made king of Judah in the south while Ish-bosheth the son of Saul was made king of Israel in the north, a hint of the division in the kingdom that will come later. Second Samuel 3:1 tells us, "There was a long war between the house of Saul and the house of David. And David grew stronger and stronger, while the house of Saul became weaker and weaker." All of the people who had followed Ish-bosheth had to decide if they would they accept the king that God had chosen and anointed and submit to his rule for their lives (which is really the same decision we have to make). When we come to 2 Samuel 5, we read:

> Then all the tribes of Israel came to David at Hebron and said, "Behold, we are your bone and flesh. In times past, when Saul was king over us, it was you who led out and brought in Israel. And the LORD said to you, 'You shall be shepherd of my people Israel, and you shall be prince over Israel.'" So all the elders of Israel came to the king at Hebron, and King David made a covenant with them at Hebron before the LORD, and they anointed David king over Israel. (vv. 5:1–3)

So then David became king over all twelve tribes. But to effectively rule over all the tribes of Israel, David needed a capital city that would be centrally located amongst the tribes, a city that could become a fortress to withstand attack. And there was such a city. In fact, it had a royal history. A thousand years before the time of David, there was a city called Salem, in which a good king named Melchizedek ruled, who was also a priest of Yahweh (Gen. 14:18). Eventually Salem was taken over by the Jebusites who built a wall around the city and called it Jebus (1 Chron. 11:4). In David's day, it was a fortress city set on a hill on the border between Judah and Benjamin, just the right location for ruling over all Israel. But there was a problem. Although it had been three hundred years since the Israelites crossed over the Jordan and began possessing the land God had promised to give to them, they still had not taken permanent possession of this great city. But this is now God's king leading God's people, and Jerusalem is about to become God's place, a city that

already had been and was going to become even more central to the
purposes of God, not only for Israel but for the world, and not just in
David's day but forever.

> And the king and his men went to Jerusalem against the Jebusites, the
> inhabitants of the land, who said to David, "You will not come in here,
> but the blind and the lame will ward you off"—thinking, "David cannot
> come in here." Nevertheless, David took the stronghold of Zion, that is,
> the city of David. (2 Sam. 5:6–7)

The stronghold on Mount Zion, one of several mountains in Jerusalem,
became the center of David's kingdom. David established his palace and
his center of government there. God established his great king in his
great city.

> And David became greater and greater, for the LORD, the God of hosts,
> was with him. And Hiram king of Tyre sent messengers to David, and
> cedar trees, also carpenters and masons who built David a house. And
> David knew that the LORD had established him king over Israel, and that
> he had exalted his kingdom for the sake of his people Israel. (2 Sam.
> 5:10–12)

David was the king, but he clearly didn't rule like other kings of his day.
Rather than ruling as a proud head of state exercising absolute control,
David ruled humbly as vice-regent to Israel's true King, God himself. He
used his throne as a pulpit from which to preach God's rule and reign.
"The LORD reigns," David wrote. "He is robed in majesty; the LORD is
robed; he has put on strength as his belt. Yes, the world is established;
it shall never be moved. Your throne is established from of old; you are
from everlasting" (Ps. 93:1–2).

The King's Joy

So David was established in Jerusalem. But there was something very
important that was not in Jerusalem. It was hidden far away. Decades
before, the ark of the covenant had been taken into battle but had been
left in the possession of the Philistines. It had been passed around from
city to city because every place the Philistines took it got struck with

plagues. So finally they took it across the border and left it in someone's home in Israel. And there it sat for decades. This meant that for decades there was no ark of the covenant in the Most Holy Place of the tabernacle for the priests to approach once a year and sprinkle with blood for the forgiveness of the people's sins. And evidently nobody seemed to care. But David cared.

In their desire for a king, the people of Israel had wanted someone to lead them into battle, and David had proved many times, over his years as a commander under Saul, that he was a great warrior. But David was not only lead warrior for Israel; he was also lead worshiper. This meant that he could not stand for the symbol of God's active presence with his people to remain far away from Jerusalem, the heart and headquarters of the people of God. David wanted to put God at the center of the city. He wanted God to be at the center of their lives.

The ark represented the throne of God, or more precisely his footstool. When David brought the ark to Jerusalem, it was his way of joining his throne to the throne of God or, more specifically, submitting his throne to the throne of God. The ark of God in the city served as a sign that David, as the king of Israel, was under the authority of the great King, that the Lord was the true king of Israel, not David. Evidently nothing could have made David happier than for his reign to derive its splendor from the presence of the ark of God.

So David had a city and a beautiful house in that city and was enjoying the presence of God with him in that city. The Philistines had been defeated, and peace had broken out all through the kingdom. After all those years of sleeping in caves and hiding from Saul and all the years of sleeping in tents on various battlefields, it must have felt good to wake up every morning in his own bed in his cedar-paneled bedroom. But one day, as David sat on the roof of his luxurious palace overlooking the city, he saw something terribly amiss. He caught a glimpse of the shabby four-hundred-year-old tent that housed the ark of God, the tabernacle. And the stark contrast between his royal dwelling and the rumpled dwelling place of the ark of God was simply embarrassing. David became determined to make things right. He wanted to do something for the God who had done so much for him.

> The king said to Nathan the prophet, "See now, I dwell in a house of cedar, but the ark of God dwells in a tent." And Nathan said to the king, "Go, do all that is in your heart, for the LORD is with you." (2 Sam. 7:1–3)

There's no indication that Nathan consulted or inquired of the Lord in this matter, as prophets were always to do before speaking with the authority of God. Evidently Nathan's first response was not formed by revelation from God but was a commonsense reaction to a good idea presented by someone whom he knew wanted to honor God.

> But that same night the word of the LORD came to Nathan, "Go and tell my servant David, 'Thus says the LORD: Would you build me a house to dwell in? I have not lived in a house since the day I brought up the people of Israel from Egypt to this day, but I have been moving about in a tent for my dwelling. In all places where I have moved with all the people of Israel, did I speak a word with any of the judges of Israel, whom I commanded to shepherd my people Israel, saying, "Why have you not built me a house of cedar?"'" (2 Sam. 7:4–7)

This was the God who comes down to dwell with his people speaking. And as long as his people were wandering, which they had done for many years in the wilderness and throughout the years of taking possession of the land in Israel, he intended to wander with them. As long as they didn't have fixed security, he was not interested in having a fixed place to dwell. Moses had told the people that when God gave them rest from all their enemies so that they were able to live in safety, then, in the place God chose, God would make his name dwell there (Deut. 12:10–11). And while there was much peace at this point under David's rule, there were still enemies to be defeated. Only when his people were settled and secure would God be ready to move out of the traveling tent and into a permanent home.

David was about to learn that "sometimes the purposes of God cut right across the desires of our hearts."[2] We have desires for things, and they are good things, even righteous things, and we are so sure that the Lord must have placed those desires in us. But we have to be careful that we are not confusing our desires with God's direction or intention.

---

[2] Iain Campbell, "Who Am I?," sermon (Point Free Church, Isle of Lewis, Scotland, October 4, 2009).

Sometimes God says no, not because he wants to deprive us or disappoint us or because what we want is sinful or bad, but because he is working out his plans for the world and for us that we cannot see from our perspective. When God's purposes cut across our desires, we can be sure that his purposes are better than ours and that his plans for our lives are better than our plans.

The King's House

Clearly God had a plan for David that exponentially surpassed any plan David could ever have conceived.

> Now, therefore, thus you shall say to my servant David, "Thus says the LORD of hosts, I took you from the pasture, from following the sheep, that you should be prince over my people Israel. And I have been with you wherever you went and have cut off all your enemies from before you. And I will make for you a great name, like the name of the great ones of the earth." (2 Sam. 7:8–9)

God honored the intention of David's heart with an intention of his own heart, saying in essence to David, "You don't provide for me; I provide for you." God doesn't operate on a quid pro quo basis but only on the basis of grace. If we think God is drumming his fingers, wishing we would come up with something creative to do for him, something impressive or costly, we have not yet understood grace. God was saying, "David, this life with me is not about *doing for* me; it is about *receiving from* me." God reminded David who is taking care of whom. God is going to make David's name great. And he's going to do more than that.

> Moreover, the LORD declares to you that the LORD will make you a house. When your days are fulfilled and you lie down with your fathers, I will raise up your offspring after you, who shall come from your body, and I will establish his kingdom. He shall build a house for my name, and I will establish the throne of his kingdom forever. I will be to him a father, and he shall be to me a son. When he commits iniquity, I will discipline him with the rod of men, with the stripes of the sons of men, but my steadfast love will not depart from him, as I took it from Saul, whom I put away from before you. (2 Sam. 7:11–15)

When David told God that he wanted to build God a house, he was talking about a temple to house the ark where the priests would offer sacrifices and mediate between God and his people. But God told David he wanted to build David a house. God wasn't talking about a family dwelling or a temple but about a royal dynasty. The British royal family, for example, is "the house of Windsor." God was promising David that his descendants would become an enduring dynasty of kings. His descendants would take his place on his throne over Israel.

The King's Throne

But this wouldn't be like any other dynasty the world had ever known.

> And your house and your kingdom shall be made sure forever before me. Your throne shall be established forever. (2 Sam. 7:16)

The blessing God promised to pour out on the world through Abraham is going to come in the form of a kingdom.

If we were identifying on a timeline of history the handful of high points, we would put our pencil point on creation and then go to the promise God made, after Adam and Eve sinned in the garden, of an offspring of the woman who would crush the Serpent's head; and then we would skip to the promise made to Abraham that all nations would be blessed through him; and then to the time when God brought Israel out of Egypt and through the Red Sea; and then our line would ark toward this day, to these promises made to David. And we would be tracing not only the significant *history* of the world; we would be discovering what we need most to know about the *future* of the world. Tracing these significant events marked by promises of blessing would help us to see that the blessing God promised to pour out on the world through Abraham is going to come in the form of a kingdom. A descendant of David is going to be the King of this kingdom. The royal Son of David is going to bless the world by ruling over it for all eternity. That is the future of the world that has been fixed by the one who created and governs this world.

To understand all that God promised here to David, we have to understand that this prophecy did what a lot of prophetic messages in the Old Testament do. It takes an extended series of events and collapses it so that the near and distant events can appear from this vantage point to be only one event. Some aspects of promises and prophecies were fulfilled in Israel's near future, and other aspects were to be fulfilled over the long-term future.

God promised that he would make David's name great and give him a place of security for his people, and he did that in David's day. God promised that he would establish a dynasty from David, that David's son would sit on his throne and would build a house for God. God did that in Solomon's day, when Solomon sat on David's throne and built a temple in Jerusalem. God promised that when David's son sinned, he would discipline him, which he did with Solomon and the other Davidic kings who followed him. But while the Davidic dynasty lasted longer than any other ancient dynasty—four hundred years— there came a day when there was no son of David sitting on the throne over God's people in Israel. In fact, there was no throne in Jerusalem and hardly a people—just a small remnant of people worshiping in a tattered temple under the rule of a foreign king. They must have wondered, and we too might wonder, what happened to God's promise that David's house, kingdom, and throne would last forever? Was the promise of forever a mirage? A failure?

In Psalm 89, a psalm written long after the days of David when it seemed as if God's commitment to the reign of his anointed king was in jeopardy, the psalmist asked the wrenching question that was likely on everyone's mind and in everyone's heart: "Lord, where is your steadfast love of old, which by your faithfulness you swore to David?" (Ps. 89:49). The psalmist was not just lamenting that there was no king and no throne; he was questioning whether God was proving faithful to his promise to David.

But while the psalmists wondered aloud about God's fulfillment of his promise, they also celebrated their certainty that their true king, God himself, was on his throne. And the prophets continually encouraged the people that God was going to do something in the future to fulfill his promise to David. Isaiah wrote: "There shall come forth a shoot from the stump of Jesse, and a branch from his roots shall bear fruit" (Isa. 11:10). Isaiah was saying that though the seed of David might have gone underground, it had not been cut off for good. Amos spoke for God, saying: "In that day I will raise up the booth of David that is fallen and repair its breaches, and raise up its ruins and rebuild it as in the days of old" (Amos 9:11). Jeremiah prophesied: "Behold, the days are coming, declares the Lord, when I will raise up for David a righteous Branch, and he shall reign as king and deal wisely, and shall execute justice and righteousness in the land (Jer. 23:5). The prophet Ezekiel wrote of a day when the exiled people of Israel would be gathered to their own land. "They and their children and their children's children shall dwell there forever, and David my servant shall be their prince forever" (Ezek. 37:25). And Zechariah seemed to see into the future by the inspiration of the Holy Spirit, saying:

> Behold, your king is coming to you;
>   righteous and having salvation is he,
> humble and mounted on a donkey,
>   on a colt, the foal of a donkey . . .
>   and he shall speak peace to the nations;
> his rule shall be from sea to sea,
>   and from the River to the ends of the earth. (Zech. 9:9–10)

Yes, the Old Testament prophets continually called the people of God to hold on to their confidence in the promises God made to David. But then the prophets stopped prophesying. There was only silence— hundreds of years of silence. But just as the death of David and all of his descendants who sat on his throne could not kill the promise, and just as the sin of David and Solomon and all of the other kings could not annul the promise, so time could not exhaust God's promise. The day came when God sent his angel Gabriel to a young girl living in Israel at a time when a cruel puppet king sat on the throne over Israel. The angel told Mary that she was going to have a son. But this wasn't going to be just any baby. This was going to be *the* Son, *the* King that generations had been longing for and waiting for ever since God made his covenant with David. The angel said:

> He will be great and will be called the Son of the Most High. And the Lord
> God will give to him the throne of his father David, and he will reign
> over the house of Jacob forever, and of his kingdom there will be no end.
> (Luke 1:32–33)

When Jesus was born in a stable in Bethlehem, the promise God made to David was fulfilled. Finally, David's son had come to take David's throne. When Jesus began his ministry and people saw his miracles, they were so astonished that they said, "Could this be the Son of David?" (Matt. 12:23). And as his ministry continued, more and more people hoped that he really would be a great warrior king like his ancestor David, one who would defeat all of their enemies. Crowds lined the street when Jesus entered into David's great city, Jerusalem, riding on a donkey, just as Zechariah had prophesied.

> So they took branches of palm trees and went out to meet him, crying out,
> "Hosanna! Blessed is he who comes in the name of the Lord, even the King
> of Israel!" (John 12:13)

But Jerusalem did not ultimately receive her King. It became clear that this King did not intend to establish a political kingdom. So instead of receiving him, they rejected him and conspired against him and handed him over to their foreign ruler, the Roman governor Pilate, to be crucified like a criminal. Rather than bowing to their King, they mocked him and spat on him. Instead of putting a crown of honor on his head, they pressed a crown of thorns into his head.

> And the soldiers twisted together a crown of thorns and put it on his head
> and arrayed him in a purple robe. They came up to him, saying, "Hail,
> King of the Jews!" and struck him with their hands . . . Pilate said to them,
> "Shall I crucify your King?" The chief priests answered, "We have no king
> but Caesar." So he delivered him over to them to be crucified. . . . Pilate also
> wrote an inscription and put it on the cross. It read, "Jesus of Nazareth, the
> King of the Jews." (John 19:2–3, 15–16, 19)

All those years of longing and waiting, and when the Son of David came, they didn't want him. Like the people of Saul's day who had wanted a warrior king who would lead them into battle, the people of

Jesus's day wanted a warrior king who would free them from the rule of Rome. But Jesus came the first time not as a warrior king but as a shepherd king—a good shepherd who laid down his life for his sheep that he might take it up again (John 10:17). Just as God had lifted David from tending sheep in Bethlehem to sit on the throne, so God raised Jesus from the grave to sit on the throne. That's where he sits now, which is what God had always intended when he put David on the throne. And evidently David knew this. The Holy Spirit revealed to David that the very purpose of David's ascension to the throne was to establish it for the Christ who would come to reign on it forever. That's what Peter said in his first sermon at Pentecost:

> Being therefore a prophet, and knowing that God had sworn with an oath to him that he would set one of his descendants on his throne, [David] foresaw and spoke about the resurrection of the Christ. . . . This Jesus God raised up, and of that we all are witnesses. Being therefore exalted at the right hand of God. . . . Let all the house of Israel therefore know for certain that God has made him both Lord and Christ, this Jesus whom you crucified. (Acts 2:29–36)

Peter made clear that not only had the Son of David come to David's city, but also, by his resurrection from the dead and his ascension to the right hand of God, he is now seated on David's throne. And because Jesus lives forever, his throne will last forever.

It wasn't long after Peter preached at Pentecost that the emperor Domitian sat on the Roman throne and demanded to be addressed as "lord" and "god." Those, like Peter, who called Jesus "Lord" and "God" were being severely persecuted and put to death. The Roman throne was a source of fear and anxiety as well as of unparalleled suffering. But the apostle John was one of many who just couldn't keep from talking about his true King, Jesus, and so he was arrested and imprisoned on Patmos. And while he was there, he was invited to see who is truly on the throne of this world, a vision he recorded in Revelation.

> I looked, and behold, a door standing open in heaven . . . . At once I was in the Spirit, and behold, a throne stood in heaven, with one seated on the throne. (Rev. 4:1–2)

As John peered into the heart of ultimate reality beyond the time and space of this world we live in now, what did he see? Amidst everything else that John saw, what stood out the most, at the center of everything, was a throne. And not just a throne, but an occupied throne, occupied by one who calls himself "the root and the descendant of David" (Rev. 22:16). There on the throne is the one who both preceded David in his deity and descended from David in his humanity.

John wrote about what he saw, pulling back the curtain for us so that we can see what is most important, what really matters. My friends, the centerpiece of heaven is not mansions with many rooms or streets of gold, though the city will be magnificent. The won-

> *The reality that all of history has been driving toward, is the son of David on the throne of the universe.*

der of heaven is not choruses of angels, though they will sound glorious. And I say this gently to those of you, who, like me, look forward with longing to seeing those you love one day in heaven: the most compelling part of heaven will not be seeing those who have gone before us. The centerpiece of heaven, the focal point of this universe, the reality that all of history has been driving toward, is the Son of David on the throne of the universe—ruling and reigning, providing a safe place for his people to rest, giving to them all the benefits of his kingdom, refusing to let anything ever harm them again.

And since Jesus is on the throne, you can stop trying to rule the world. You can stop all of your worrying and your vain attempts to control everything about your life and your family. The one who is seated on the throne is not only able to supply your needs and provide your protection; he has at his disposal everything needed to fulfill all of his promises to you. Because he is on the throne, your joy doesn't have to be so tied to your circumstances, and your sense of security doesn't have to be so easily shaken. The Lord reigns.

The latest report on cable news about the state of the world does not define the future. That's why we probably shouldn't begin our days with the morning news on the television or radio or Internet. Instead, we should begin in the Word of God. Every day should begin and end by being reminded from the Scriptures: *The Lord God Omnipotent reigns. He reigns over my difficult circumstances. He reigns over my ongoing conflict. He reigns over my carefully crafted plans. And he can be trusted. He is a good King.*

The Lord who reigns is so good that he actually invites us to approach his throne with the confidence that, when we do, we will not be shamed or condemned or turned away. Instead, we will find grace and mercy. We can pour out all of our concerns to him who sits on the throne, saying, "Jesus, you are king over all of this. Forgive me for feeling so free to question you, blame you, even disregard you. Give me eyes to see you on your throne. Give me a heart willing to trust that you will do what is best. Give me the spiritual strength to bend to your righteous rule in my life. Help me to live out this day in peace, confident that you are on your throne."

We can live this way today because we know there is a day coming, a day when our ears will hear what John's ears heard. On that day, we will enter the New Jerusalem. The presence of God will be there radiating the glory that will penetrate into the deepest part of us. There in the center will be the throne occupied by the Son of David. We'll hear loud voices saying, "The kingdom of the world has become the kingdom of our Lord and of his Christ, and he shall reign forever and ever" (Rev. 11:15). And it will be the best news we've ever heard.

This world—your world—is not ruled by the forces of random chance. King Jesus is on his throne. And he will reign forever and ever.

> Crown Him with many crowns, The Lamb upon His throne.
> Hark! How the heav'nly anthem drowns all music but its own!
> Awake, my soul, and sing of Him who died for thee,
> And hail Him as thy matchless King through all eternity.[3]

---

[3] Matthew Bridges, "Crown Him with Many Crowns," 1852.

Looking Forward

Disturbed No More

In the promise God made to David, we find some elements that were fulfilled in David's day, some that were fulfilled in Solomon's day, and some that were fulfilled in Jesus's day. But there are also some aspects to the promise that still have not been completely fulfilled. God promised David:

> I will appoint a place for my people Israel and will plant them, so that they may dwell in their own place and be disturbed no more. And violent men shall afflict them no more, as formerly, from the time that I appointed judges over my people Israel. And I will give you rest from all your enemies. (2 Sam. 7:10–11)

Surely these promises were partially fulfilled when David defeated all of the threats around Israel and even more when the people of Israel lived in abundant peace and prosperity during Solomon's reign (1 Kings 4:24). But though Israel had been planted in the borders of Israel, they were once again disturbed. Violent men did afflict them again. Only five years after Solomon's death, the king of Egypt invaded Judah and Israel. Though they were given rest for a while, it didn't last. The people of God continued to long for the king who would ascend to David's throne and bring the peace that God had promised; the person and the peace that Isaiah prophesied was still to come:

> For to us a child is born,
> to us a son is given;
> and the government shall be upon his shoulder,
> and his name shall be called
> Wonderful Counselor, Mighty God,
> Everlasting Father, Prince of Peace.
> Of the increase of his government and of peace
> there will be no end,
> on the throne of David and over his kingdom,
> to establish it and to uphold it

with justice and with righteousness
    from this time forth and forevermore.
The zeal of the LORD of hosts will do this. (Isa. 9:6–7)

Jesus is the ultimate fulfillment of the child who was born, the
son who was given. But when he came the first time, did he usher in
the era of peace and absence of conflict that was promised to David
and prophesied by Isaiah? Clearly when he came the first time, he
came to do battle with the ancient enemy of God's people, a decisive
battle that took place outside the city gates of Jerusalem, accomplishing a victory evidenced by an empty grave. But where is the peace that
was promised? Where is the peace of which there will be no end? Anyone who lives in this world of conflict and catastrophe knows that we
cannot be living in the reality of all that God promised to his people.

So what do we do with God's promise to David and to his people of
being disturbed and afflicted no more? If we think about it, we realize
that the "no more" aspects of the promise to David remind us of the
way the apostle John described Jerusalem—not the Jerusalem of David's or Solomon's day, and certainly not the Jerusalem of Jesus's day,
but the new Jerusalem coming out of heaven from God.

And I heard a loud voice from the throne saying, "Behold, the
dwelling place of God is with man. He will dwell with them, and
they will be his people, and God himself will be with them as their
God. He will wipe away every tear from their eyes, and death shall
be no more, neither shall there be mourning, nor crying, nor pain
anymore, for the former things have passed away." (Rev. 21:3–4)

The day will come when all of those who have gladly bowed the
knee to King Jesus will enter into his great city, where we will dwell
forever with him. We will no longer be disturbed by anxious thoughts or
petty jealousies or selfish desires. We will no longer be afflicted by natural disasters or deadly viruses or defective genes. This will be the final
and complete rest from all our enemies that God's people have been
longing for and looking forward to ever since God made his promise to
David. Our Prince of Peace will be on the throne in the center of the city,
and of the increase of his government and of peace there will be no end.

Discussion Guide

2 Samuel

Getting the Discussion Going

1. As humans, we are bound by time. It is hard for us to wrap our minds around "forever." But as you think about what this lesson reveals about the kind of forever God has in mind for us, what does that make you think, and how does that make you feel?

Getting to the Heart of It

2. When the tribes of Israel came to David at Hebron, they acknowledged the truth that long ago God had said that David would be the shepherd and prince over Israel. Yet for many years they had been resisting David's kingship. How is this a picture of the way many people respond to King Jesus? (See Rom. 1:18–21.)

3. 2 Samuel 5:12 says, "And David knew that the LORD had established him king over Israel, and that he had exalted his kingdom for the sake of his people Israel." What difference do you think this knowledge made in how David ruled?

4. What do you think about David's desire and Nathan's initial response in 2 Samuel 7:1–3? What was the basis for them? What was problematic with them?

5. Read together David's prayer in 2 Samuel 7:18–29, which was offered in response to the promises God had made to him. What are some things that stand out to you in this prayer? What evidence do you see that David truly is a man after God's heart, the kind of king God wants to have on the throne over his people?

6. Look back at the chart you filled out in the Personal Bible Study in regard to the promises God made to David and how they were fulfilled or will be fulfilled. Which one did you find especially interesting or meaningful?

Getting Personal

7. As you think about what it means that King Jesus is on the throne now until all of his enemies are put under his feet and that he will be on the throne of the universe into eternity with all of his enemies gone forever, what comfort does it bring you? What challenge does it present to you?

Getting How It Fits into the Big Picture

8. When we trace God's promise of blessing from the garden of Eden to the promise to bless Abraham and on to God's promise to David, how does it help us to understand why the New Testament begins by giving us the genealogy that demonstrates that Jesus was a descendant of David?

1 Kings

Personal Bible Study

1 Kings

1. In 1 Kings 2:1–4 we read the instructions David gave to Solomon for ruling as king over Israel as well as a description of the blessings Solomon would enjoy if he ruled in this way. What are the key things David told Solomon to do, and what could he expect if he did these things?

2. Read 1 Kings 3:1–3. We can see right away that the writer of 1 Kings is not going to whitewash Solomon's story. Here at the outset we see that Solomon is a mix of good and bad (just as we are). What do you see here that bodes well for the future of his reign as king, and what causes concern? (See Deut. 12:2–5 and 17:16 for assistance.)

3. Read 1 Kings 3:4–9. What do you see about how Solomon sees himself and what he desires?

4. Read 1 Kings 3:10–15. How did God respond to Solomon's request?

5. Read 1 Kings 3:16–29. How does this story of the two prostitutes who came before Solomon illustrate that God has indeed given Solomon what he asked for?

6. Read 1 Kings 4:20–25. Solomon had expressed concern that he did not have the ability to govern God's people. But what are the signs that God has given him the wisdom to do so?

7. Read 1 Kings 4:29–34. In addition to wisdom for governing, in what other matters was Solomon given wisdom?

8. As Solomon procured the materials and began to build a house for the Lord, once again the word of the Lord came to him with a command and a promise, which is recorded in 1 Kings 6:11–13. What was the command and the blessing promised for obedience to the command?

9. Remember that Adam and Eve had been ejected from the garden of Eden because of their disobedience, and that God, in redemption history, is working out his plan to bring his people back into his land where he will dwell with them. Read the description in 1 Kings 6:14–38 of the temple Solomon built. What do you see in the details of the design of the temple that are reminiscent of Eden?

10. The most wonderful thing about the temple is told in 1 Kings 8:10–11. What is it?

11. Solomon responded to the Lord's filling of the temple with his glory by blessing the Lord, praying a beautiful prayer of dedication, and giving the people a charge, which is recorded in 1 Kings 8:12–61. Read or skim this blessing, prayer, and charge and note two or three things that stand out to you.

12. Read 1 Kings 10:1–13. The queen of Sheba came to test Solomon with hard questions. Use your imagination for a minute and list three or four questions you think she might have asked him.

13. The queen of Sheba was breathless and amazed by the wisdom of Solomon as well as by the temple he had built, the government he had organized, the food he served, and the way he worshiped. What did she do in response, according to verses 9–10?

14. As wise as Solomon was, there continued to be signs of problems. We saw earlier that he went back to Egypt and took a foreign wife and accommodated worship in the high places. In 1 Kings 10 and 11, we find evidence of further disobedience. Compare the commandment for Israel's king, given in Deuteronomy 17, with what Solomon did, recorded in the following verses.

Requirements for Israel's kings	Solomon's disobedience as king
[He shall not] acquire for himself excessive silver and gold. (Deut. 17:17)	1 Kings 10:14–21
He must not acquire many horses for himself. (Deut. 17:16)	1 Kings 10:26
He shall not acquire many wives for himself, lest his heart turn away. (Deut. 17:17)	1 Kings 11:3

15. Read 1 Kings 3:3 and compare it to 1 Kings 11:1–4. What has happened?

16. According to 1 Kings 11:5–8, how was Solomon's change in heart evidenced in what he did?

17. Read 1 Kings 11:9–14, 23, and 26. What was God's response to Solomon's heart turning away from him and toward other gods?

Teaching Chapter

Something Greater

For some, the past has a special allure. We remember or read about a time in history that seems idyllic to us and wish we could have lived then. That's how it was for Gil, a disenchanted Hollywood screenwriter played by Owen Wilson in the film *Midnight in Paris*. Gil dreams about escaping his unsatisfying present reality to live in Paris in the 1920s. And through the magic of the movies, he gets to experience it. He is picked up at the stroke of midnight by an antique car and taken back in time. There he runs into Scott and Zelda Fitzgerald at an elegant soiree. He hears Cole Porter crooning, gets writing advice from Hemingway, and persuades Gertrude Stein to read the manuscript of his novel. He also falls in love with Picasso's mistress, Adriana, who has her own golden-era fantasies. To Adriana, the best time to be alive would have been the Belle Époque, the pre–World War I era when peace and prosperity in Paris allowed the arts to flourish. But when Adriana takes Gil back in time to this idealized time, he is not impressed. He sees the downside. "These people don't have any antibiotics!" he says. And, personally, I think he has a very good point.

Similarly, the Israelites in Jesus's day had an era they looked back on, a time they longed to return to, an era in their history when everything was as it should be. During the reign of King Solomon, everything God had promised to Abraham came together in their experience. They were a people as numerous as the sand on the shore and the stars in the sky. They were at peace, living in the land God had promised under the wisest king ever known. They were experiencing the blessing of God in abundant crops and increasing wealth. Their very existence was a blessing to the world around them as all the kings of the earth were in awe of the glory of Israel's king and kingdom. And best of all, God's promise to be their God and to dwell among them had become a reality. God had descended in a cloud of glory to make his home in the magnificent temple at the center of their city.

This, indeed, was a time worthy of looking back at and longing for. It was wonderful, but there was a problem. It didn't last. It all fell apart. The kingdom was torn in two, the wealth was carried away, the borders were invaded, the kings were disgraced, and the temple was burned. The prophets spoke of a day in the future when the kingdom would be restored. And so God's people waited and wished for the kingdom to be restored to what it was in the days of Solomon and for a king to come who would be what Solomon once was.

Nine hundred years later there came a carpenter's son from the town of Nazareth. He was wholly unimpressive, a man who didn't even own a home, let alone a palace. But when he spoke, he seemed wiser than their greatest wisdom teachers. He spoke of the zenith of Israel's history, when the kingdom of Israel was at its peak in terms of wealth and power and territory and peace and security, the era that generations looked back at longingly. And then he said something shocking. He said, "Something greater than Solomon is here" (Matt. 12:42). A king greater and wiser than Solomon? A kingdom with more abundance and grandeur than that of Israel in Solomon's day? Those who heard him must have said to themselves, "What is he talking about? Who is this king, and where is this kingdom?"

That is the question we want to answer. But if we truly want to grasp this greater King and this greater kingdom, first we need to understand what was so great about Solomon and the kingdom of Israel in his day. So we turn to 1 Kings, where we learn about the wonders of Solomon's wisdom, wealth, and worship.

Solomon's Wisdom

First Kings begins with the death of King David in the time before the temple was built in Jerusalem. Solomon has taken his place on the throne. In chapter 3 we read that Solomon has gone to Gibeon, where the tabernacle had come to rest, to offer sacrifices. And there God came down to open up the world to him.

> At Gibeon the LORD appeared to Solomon in a dream by night, and God said, "Ask what I shall give you." (1 Kings 3:5)

This was much more than a generous invitation. It was also a significant test. As the newly enthroned king, Solomon might want to ask for victory over his enemies or success in his endeavors or money in his coffers. But that is not what Solomon asked for.

> O LORD my God, you have made your servant king in place of David my father, although I am but a little child. I do not know how to go out or come in. And your servant is in the midst of your people whom you have chosen, a great people, too many to be numbered or counted for multitude. Give your servant therefore *an understanding mind to govern* your people, that I may discern between good and evil, for who is able to govern this your great people? (1 Kings 3:5–9)

Solomon's response to God's offer revealed that Solomon saw himself as a partaker in the covenant promises of God. It also revealed a child-like dependence upon God, a recognition that he did not know how to rule over God's people, but he wanted to do it well. Solomon asked specifically for "an understanding mind to govern" so that he could "discern between good and evil." Immediately we are told a story that is meant to show us that this prayer was answered. When two prostitutes both claimed to be the mother of one living baby and stood before Solomon making their case, Solomon demonstrated that God had indeed given him the divine ability to discern good and evil. Everyone must have been horrified when Solomon called for a sword to cut the living baby in two. But in great wisdom Solomon had devised this test to reveal the secret motivations in the hearts of the two mothers. And when he put the baby into the true mother's arms, everyone was amazed so that "all Israel heard of the judgment that the king had rendered, and they stood in awe of the king, because they perceived that the wisdom of God was in him to do justice" (1 Kings 3:28).

If you have ever spent any time in a country in which corruption is woven into the fabric of all of society and government so that citizens have no confidence that justice will be done, perhaps you have a special ability to appreciate what it means to have a government with the wisdom and the will to execute justice. Remember that this was a land in which "everyone did what was right in his own eyes" for centuries. But now a king is on the throne who has the wisdom to discern between good and evil and the power to enact justice. This was a good time to be living in Israel, under this wise king.

> Judah and Israel were as many as the sand by the sea. They ate and drank and were happy. . . . For he had dominion over all the region west of the Euphrates from Tiphsah to Gaza, over all the kings west of the Euphrates. And he had peace on all sides around him. And Judah and Israel lived in safety, from Dan even to Beersheba, every man under his vine and under his fig tree, all the days of Solomon. (1 Kings 4:20, 24–25)

The farms throughout Israel are yielding harvests, and everyone is feasting. Their ancestors once groaned and cried out under cruel bondage in Egypt, but now they are enjoying all God had promised to their father Abraham so long ago. There is every reason to be happy—God is proving true to all of his promises. They're all being fulfilled. Husbands and sons are no longer going out to war. Life is good. And their king? Well, he's amazing.

> He also spoke 3,000 proverbs, and his songs were 1,005. He spoke of trees, from the cedar that is in Lebanon to the hyssop that grows out of the wall. He spoke also of beasts, and of birds, and of reptiles, and of fish. And people of all nations came to hear the wisdom of Solomon, and from all the kings of the earth, who had heard of his wisdom. (1 Kings 4:32–34)

Evidently Solomon was a Renaissance man long before the Renaissance. He was a philosopher, a political scientist, an engineer, and an architect—as well as a songwriter. He would have set a new record for wins on *Jeopardy* and taken home the prize on *Who Wants to Be a Millionaire?* without using any lifelines. He would have gotten a Grammy for songwriter of the year. He would have had millions of people following his Proverbs Twitter feed. Everyone in the world wanted to hear what he had to say about anything and everything—including the queen of a foreign country far to the east.

> Now when the queen of Sheba heard of the fame of Solomon concerning the name of the LORD, she came to test him with hard questions. She came to Jerusalem with a very great retinue, with camels bearing spices and very much gold and precious stones. And when she came to Solomon, she told him all that was on her mind. And Solomon answered all her questions; there was nothing hidden from the king that he could not explain to her. And when the queen of Sheba had seen all the wisdom of Solomon, the house that he had built, the food of his table, the seating of his officials, and the attendance of his servants, their clothing, his cupbearers, and his burnt offerings that he offered at the house of the LORD, there was no more breath in her. (1 Kings 10:1–5)

She has some hard questions—questions no one else she knows has been able to answer. I wonder what her questions were. Did she want to have her questions about planting and harvesting answered so that the farmers in her country could grow more hearty crops? Did she want to have her questions about running a kingdom answered so she could go back and make some changes in her government? Did she come with questions about the God of Abraham, Isaac, and Jacob, wanting to know why he had brought his people out of slavery and into this land and blessed them? Did she ask Solomon about the identity of the seed of the woman who would one day come and crush the head of the Serpent, putting an end to the evil and suffering that makes life in a broken world so difficult? Did she ask him to explain the real meaning behind animal sacrifice? Whatever her questions were, Solomon answered them, leaving her breathless.

Solomon was the wisest of wise men so that the whole world came to learn from him. Yet we will see that Solomon also exhibited great foolishness. There was a limit to his wisdom, a failure in his wisdom. Someone with greater wisdom would be needed to sit on David's throne over God's people.

Solomon's Wealth

Along with the unprecedented wisdom that made Solomon the wisest man in the world, God also gave Solomon unparalleled wealth, making him the richest man in the world. Try to grasp the impression that the writer of 1 Kings is trying to make on us, the readers, regarding Solomon's wealth.

> Now the weight of gold that came to Solomon in one year was 666 talents of gold, besides that which came from the explorers and from the business of the merchants, and from all the kings of the west and from the governors of the land. King Solomon made 200 large shields of beaten gold; 600 shekels of gold went into each shield. And he made 300 shields of beaten gold; three minas of gold went into each shield. And the king put them in the House of the Forest of Lebanon. The king also made a great ivory throne and overlaid it with the finest gold. . . . All King Solomon's drinking vessels were of gold, and all the vessels of the House of the Forest of Lebanon were of pure gold. None were of silver; silver was not considered as anything in the days of Solomon. For the king had a fleet of ships of Tarshish at sea with the fleet of Hiram. Once every three years the fleet of ships of Tarshish used to come bringing gold, silver, ivory, apes, and peacocks. (1 Kings 10:14–18, 21)

Are you getting the picture from the repetition of the word "gold"? The writer is trying to impress upon us the incredible wealth of Solomon's kingdom. Today his gold would be melted into bars and stacked in a vault, but in Solomon's day gold was fashioned into ceremonial shields. And there were hundreds of them littered around Solomon's palace. But, sadly, this abundance of gold in the kingdom of Israel did not last long past Solomon's life. We read about that later in 1 Kings, in the days after Solomon died.

> In the fifth year of King Rehoboam, Shishak king of Egypt came up against Jerusalem. He took away the treasures of the house of the LORD and the treasures of the king's house. He took away everything. He also took away all the shields of gold that Solomon had made. (1 Kings 14:25–26)

In just one generation all the gold was gone. Clearly needed was a wealth that is invulnerable to poor investment or invading armies, a wealth that is reserved and preserved where neither moth nor rust destroys and where thieves do not break in and steal (Matt. 6:20).

Solomon's Worship

So 1 Kings reveals to us the wisdom and wealth of Solomon. It also shows us Solomon's heart for worship as evidenced by his desire and determination to build a magnificent temple. Ever since God had called Abraham and blessed

> *The golden splendor of the temple was made glorious by the presence of God himself.*

him and promised to be his God, the history of God's people had been driving toward the day when God's people would live securely in God's place where God would live among them and they would worship and serve him.

Chapter 5 details the procurement of building materials and labor for the building project. No effort or expense was spared. Chapter 6 describes in intricate detail the design for the temple, which was meant to remind God's people of Eden. When a priest came to the door of Solomon's temple, he saw "carvings of cherubim, palm trees, and open flowers" (1 Kings 6:32, 35), and it was if he were coming to the gates of paradise. No wonder the people of Israel in the generations to come longed for the temple and the kingdom to be restored to its former glory. It was the closest thing to paradise they had ever known.

When the ark of the covenant was placed in the temple, the temple became what Solomon had built it to be: not just a beautiful building but the center of his people's worship, the earthly dwelling place for the true and living God.

> And when the priests came out of the Holy Place, a cloud filled the house of the LORD, so that the priests could not stand to minister because of the cloud, for the glory of the LORD filled the house of the LORD. (1 Kings 8:10–11)

The golden splendor of the temple was made glorious by the presence of God himself. Yahweh, the maker of heaven and earth, settled in Jerusalem where he could hear his people's prayers and capture his people's hearts. But his desires were not aimed only at the Israelites. The temple in Jerusalem was home base from which God would accomplish his intention to make the glory of his name known throughout the entire earth to all the peoples of the earth.

When the Lord that Solomon loved moved into the house that Solomon built, Solomon broke out in one of the most beautiful prayers in the Bible, asking God to listen to his people's prayers and to forgive. Then, once again, the Lord appeared to Solomon with a promise and a warning.

> And the LORD said to him, "I have heard your prayer and your plea, which you have made before me. I have consecrated this house that you have built, by putting my name there forever. My eyes and my heart will be there for all time. And as for you, if you will walk before me, as David your father walked, with integrity of heart and uprightness, doing according to all that I have commanded you, and keeping my statutes and my rules, then I will establish your royal throne over Israel forever, as I promised David your father, saying, 'You shall not lack a man on the throne of Israel.' But if you turn aside from following me, you or your children, and do not keep my commandments and my statutes that I have set before you, but go and serve other gods and worship them, then I will cut off Israel from the land that I have given them, and the house that I have consecrated for my name I will cast out of my sight, and Israel will become a proverb and a byword among all peoples. And this house will become a heap of ruins." (1 Kings 9:3–8)

While the Lord's presence among his people had been contingent on the nation of Israel's faithfulness under Moses, now that Israel had a king, the Lord's presence became contingent on the faithfulness of Israel's king. And sadly Israel's kings were not faithful. The temple that Solomon built was glorious and beautiful. But the day came when it was made desolate and brought down to destruction. It was stripped of all its golden splendor and became an empty building where God could no longer dwell. Clearly, a greater, more glorious, more permanent temple was needed, a temple in which the glory of God was pleased to dwell.

Solomon's Wives

So Solomon was great in his wisdom and his wealth and his worship. But all was not well behind the scenes of splendor. The writer of 1 Kings has stated the facts without comment along the way lest we think there has been an effort to conceal the truth. There have been hints all along in 1 Kings that we could have picked up on.

First was the alliance Solomon made with Egypt by marrying the daughter of Pharaoh, even though God had commanded Israel's kings not to return to Egypt (1 Kings 3:1; Deut. 17:16). Then there was the offering of sacrifices at the high places, even though God had commanded Israel to destroy the high places (1 Kings 3:3; Deut. 12:2–5). And now, in chapter 11, the writer of 1 Kings comes out and summarizes what has been developing throughout Solomon's life in spite of God's gracious gift of wisdom:

> Now King Solomon loved many foreign women, along with the daughter of Pharaoh: Moabite, Ammonite, Edomite, Sidonian, and Hittite women, from the nations concerning which the LORD had said to the people of Israel, "You shall not enter into marriage with them, neither shall they with you, for surely they will *turn away* your heart after their gods." Solomon clung to these in love. He had 700 wives, who were princesses, and 300 concubines. And his wives *turned away* his heart. For when Solomon was old his wives *turned away* his heart after other gods, and his heart was not wholly true to the LORD his God, as was the heart of David his father. (1 Kings 11:1–4)

The same heart that was filled with wisdom and made discerning by God has turned away after other gods. At the beginning of Solomon's story in 1 Kings 3:3, we read that "Solomon loved the LORD," something not said about any other person in the Bible. But here at the end of his story we read that Solomon "loved many foreign women" and that "his heart was not wholly true to the LORD his God." Clearly, a dramatic change has taken place in Solomon's affections. When we read that Solomon clung to these women in love, the author is presenting to us the picture of a pathetic old man with a bad toupee and gold chains around his neck taking exotic young women on overnight jaunts on his yacht. These are royal daughters of the very nations that God had told Israel to drive out of the Promised Land. Yet Solomon is foolishly giving his heart to them and welcoming them into the palace. Even worse, he is worshiping their gods.

> For Solomon went after Ashtoreth the goddess of the Sidonians, and after
> Milcom the abomination of the Ammonites. So Solomon did what was
> evil in the sight of the LORD and did not wholly follow the LORD, as David
> his father had done. Then Solomon built a high place for Chemosh the
> abomination of Moab, and for Molech the abomination of the Ammonites,
> on the mountain east of Jerusalem. And so he did for all his foreign wives,
> who made offerings and sacrificed to their gods. (1 Kings 11:5–8)

Solomon *went after* Ashtoreth the goddess of the Sidonians. Solomon *went after* Milcom the abomination of the Ammonites. Perhaps this doesn't shock us because we don't really understand what it meant for him to "go after" these gods. We don't have any mental pictures. Ashtoreth was the Canaanite goddess of sensual love and fertility. To go after this god meant that Solomon likely went to the high places and had sexual relations out in the open with temple prostitutes. Milcom, the god of the Ammonites, was worshiped through child sacrifice, so we have to assume that perhaps Solomon lowered himself to throwing one of his children into the fire to appease this false god out of desperation to please some Ammonite wife. Solomon put a shrine for Molech right on the Mount of Olives, in clear view from the temple. When he worshiped at this shrine it was like saying, "In your face," to the God who had been so very generous and gracious to him.

Surely if we had lived in Solomon's day—if we had witnessed one of his wise rulings or taken a tour of his house and gardens or listened to one of his lectures—we would have walked away quite sure that he would be the last person in the world to fall into serious sin. He looked so good. He made God look so good. He brought blessing to so many. He was able to explain things no one else could. He would have been the go-to guy for advice on how to deal with our most perplexing situations. But then we discover that something has been going on in his life that causes us to question our easy admiration for him. For all of the peace and security and abundance that he brought to his people, we see that he also brought disaster upon them. How can this be? How could someone given so much wisdom succumb to such foolishness?

Honestly, this is something I have struggled with in regard to Solomon's story. Here is this man to whom God has given extraordinary wisdom—wisdom for living in the world God has made under his rule—and yet he seems so foolish. It's hard for me to understand. I was talking about this with my husband, David, and I said, "I guess he just made a lot of little compromises along the way that turned his heart away from God." And David said, "But they weren't *little* compromises. They were enormous."

Yes, I realized. *They were.* And perhaps that reveals the real issue. Surely they seemed small to him at the time. Maybe he justified taking so many foreign wives as a strategic way to ensure the security of the kingdom. Maybe he justified building altars for the false gods of these wives under the guise of being a good husband. Maybe he justi-

> *Solomon loved the Lord. But he also had some other loves in his life— loves that crowded out the place in his heart that should have been reserved for God alone.*

fied procuring many horses and chariots assuming that when Moses gave instructions for Israel's kings not to do so, he just didn't anticipate the current culture. Perhaps he intended to use the platform his fame provided for him to be salt and light in the world—only to end up being corrupted by the world.

Solomon loved the Lord. But he also had some other loves in his life—loves that crowded out the place in his heart that should have been reserved for God alone. And as I say it I realize that it isn't really so hard to understand, because I have other loves in my life that threaten to crowd out the place in my heart that should be reserved for God alone.

Solomon was a success at international trade. He was a success at completing huge building projects. He had power over his people, a royal navy, an enormous treasury, an impressive reputation. But somewhere along the way he became a failure in what matters most: his exclusive love relationship with the living God. Perhaps this is why the writer of Hebrews admonishes us, "Take care, brothers, lest there be in any of you an evil, unbelieving heart, leading you to fall away from the living God" (Heb. 3:12).

The kingdom in the days of Solomon was glorious. But it didn't last because the heart of the king did not stay true. His heart was divided.

And so was the kingdom. Never again was the kingdom in Israel as glorious as it was under Solomon, though the Israelites longed for it to be restored. They believed that when Messiah came, he would restore the kingdom of Israel to the glory it once had in the days of Solomon.

Solomon's Greater Son

And then Jesus showed up saying that "something greater than Solomon is here." Just how were Jesus and the kingdom he brings greater?

While Solomon was the wisest man in the world in his time, in Jesus are hidden "all the treasure of wisdom and knowledge" (Col. 2:30). We think it is just too simplistic to say that Jesus is the answer to our deep philosophical questions and complex relational issues. But the Bible tells us that he "became to us wisdom from God" (1 Cor. 1:30). We need the wisdom that is Christ to supplant the wisdom of the world that has permeated our perspectives.

While Solomon loved the Lord, Jesus is the only person who has ever loved the Lord with all of his heart, mind, and strength without fail. The reality is that you and I cannot be totally consecrated or wholeheartedly devoted to God on our own. But Jesus has invited us to be joined to him so that through him, we who have been unfaithful can be made perfectly and enduringly faithful.

While Solomon accumulated riches, Jesus became poor. "For you know the grace of our Lord Jesus Christ, that though he was rich, yet for your sake he became poor, so that you by his poverty might become rich" (2 Cor. 8:9). We have been made rich in salvation benefits because Jesus impoverished himself on the cross.

While Solomon exercised justice, Jesus endured injustice. There on the cross between two thieves, one of them recognized this, saying, "We are receiving the due reward of our deeds; but this man has done nothing wrong" (Luke 23:41). He recognized that Jesus was indeed a greater King over a greater kingdom and said to him, "Jesus, remember me when you come into your kingdom" (v. 42).

While Solomon drafted a great labor force to accomplish all of his building projects, King Jesus came not to be served but to serve, saying, "Whoever would be great among you must be your servant" (Matt. 20:26).

While Solomon ushered in an era of peace for Israel with her enemies, Jesus makes it possible for enemies of God to have peace with God. "For in him all the fullness of God was pleased to dwell, and through him to reconcile to himself all things, whether on earth or in heaven, making peace by the blood of his cross" (Col. 1:19–20).

While Solomon built a temple that was eventually torn down, Jesus is the temple who was raised up. "Destroy this temple, and in three days I will raise it up," he said (John 2:19), which is just what he did when he rose from the grave.

While Solomon reigned over the entire territory of Israel, Jesus reigns over the entire universe. He told the disciples, "All authority in heaven and on earth has been given to me." (Matt. 28:18)

While Solomon had many wives, Jesus has only one bride. He loves her and gave himself up for her. He has no intention of accommodating her worship of other gods but has cleansed her so that she might be holy and without blemish (Eph. 5:25–27).

The people of God looked back at the era of Israel under Solomon and longed for things to be the way they once were. Yet when we read the story of Solomon, we're not meant to long for what was. Instead we're meant to take it in as a picture of what will be. Something greater came when Jesus became flesh and dwelt among us. But there is something even greater yet to come. We're getting tastes and glimpses of it now as citizens of heaven, and the day will come when this kingdom will become the reality that we will live in forever. The day will come when we will stand before our greater King and say to him the words spoken to King Solomon by the queen of Sheba. We'll say to King Jesus: "Happy are your men! Happy are your servants, who continually stand before you and hear your wisdom! Blessed be the LORD your God, who has delighted in you and set you on the throne of Israel! Because the LORD loved Israel forever, he has made you king, that you may execute justice and righteousness" (1 Kings 10:8–9).

Looking Forward

The Kings of the Earth Will Bring Their Glory into It

Throughout the 1 Kings account of the kingdom under Solomon, our eyes are drawn to the procession of royalty from other nations paying tribute and expressing wonder at the kingdom God established in Israel and the king he put on the throne.

> And people of all nations came to hear the wisdom of Solomon, and from all the kings of the earth, who had heard of his wisdom. (1 Kings 4:34)

We also read the account of one royal visitor in particular, the queen of Sheba, who came to see Solomon, bringing not only her questions but a wealth of gifts.

> Then she gave the king 120 talents of gold, and a very great quantity of spices and precious stones. Never again came such an abundance of spices as these that the queen of Sheba gave to King Solomon. Moreover, the fleet of Hiram, which brought gold from Ophir, brought from Ophir a very great amount of almug wood and precious stones. (1 Kings 10:10–11)

This is an amazing detail—that Gentile kings brought gifts to God's king that were used to build the temple where the living God would dwell and be worshiped. This was a living picture of people from every tribe and tongue and nation being grafted in, becoming a part of God's great purposes. It was also a preview of something that would happen centuries later.

> Now after Jesus was born in Bethlehem of Judea in the days of Herod the king, behold, wise men from the east came to Jerusalem, saying, "Where is he who has been born king of the Jews?" . . . And going into the house they saw the child with Mary his mother, and they fell down and worshiped him. Then, opening their treasures, they offered him gifts, gold and frankincense and myrrh. (Matt. 2:1–2, 11)

Once again, royalty from the east was drawn to come into the earthly kingdom of God to worship the King God had sent to take the throne of David. But this, too, points to something greater yet to come. This was not the last time kings from the earth will come to bring honor to God's chosen King. The day will come in the New Jerusalem when Gentile kings from the earth will stream into the city of our God to pay homage to the King. John saw a vision of that day.

> And I saw no temple in the city, for its temple is the Lord God the Almighty and the Lamb. And the city has no need of sun or moon to shine on it, for the glory of God gives it light, and its lamp is the Lamb. By its light will the nations walk, and the kings of the earth will bring their glory into it, and its gates will never be shut by day—and there will be no night there. They will bring into it the glory and the honor of the nations. (Rev. 21:22–26)

All of the great treasures of the cultures and kingdoms of this present earth will flow into the kingdom of God in the new heaven and the new earth. The distinctions of different peoples and cultures will not be removed; they will be redeemed, all for the glory of God's great King, the Son of David.

Discussion Guide

1 Kings

Getting the Discussion Going

1. Think back on the descriptions of Solomon and the life his people enjoyed in his kingdom. What are some of the things they enjoyed that they never had before?

Getting to the Heart of It

2. Solomon is the only man in the entire Bible of whom it is said that he loved the Lord. Think about that. David wasn't described that way. Daniel wasn't described that way. John the Baptist wasn't described that way. Why do you think this is said of Solomon?

3. First Kings makes it clear that Solomon was the wisest man in the world and the richest man in the world and had more honor than any king in the world in his day. And Jesus announced that "something greater than Solomon is here." How would you explain what he meant?

4. In the Personal Bible Study questions, you were asked to note several things that stood out to you in Solomon's blessing, dedication prayer, and charge to the people after the Lord filled the temple with his glory (1 Kings 8). What was significant to you?

5. While the writer of 1 Kings tells us that Solomon loved the Lord, and we get to read his beautiful prayer, there is no record of him ever reading and studying the commandments of the Lord in the law of Moses, which he was instructed to follow. How might that have made a difference, and what does this teach us if we want to avoid having our hearts turned away from God toward other loves?

6. Read Matthew 12:42 in light of the account in 1 Kings 10 of the queen of Sheba's response to Solomon and his God. What was Jesus saying in regard to why the queen of Sheba will "rise up at the judgment with this generation and condemn it"?

7. We are horrified when we picture in our minds what Solomon must have done when he went after other gods. But certainly there are things we do in going after our idols that should shock us. Work your way through the following idols of our age and suggest some ways we "go after" these gods.

- the idol of financial security
- the idol of physical beauty and eternal youth
- the idol of fame and reputation
- the idol of the perfect family
- the idol of power in business or politics or even in the church

Getting Personal

8. The writer seems to be indicating an exception to Solomon's love for the Lord and walking in the statutes of David in 1 Kings 3:3 when he adds: *only* or *except* that he offered sacrifices at the "high places." Solomon loved the Lord, *except* . . . What is it that might fill in the "only" or "except" clause in the account of your life? Or could it be said of you that you loved the Lord with no exceptions?

Getting How It Fits into the Big Picture

9. Throughout this study we're seeking to discover how each part of Israel's history fits into the bigger story. How would you connect this history of the kingdom of Israel under Solomon to each of the following: the way things were in the garden of Eden, the promises made to Abraham, the first coming of Christ, and the second coming of Christ?

Week 8

2 Kings

Personal Bible Study

2 Kings

In the centuries leading up to the era of the divided kingdoms of Israel and Judah, God had repeatedly warned his people about what would happen if they disobeyed him and turned to other gods. The covenant God made with the nation of Israel at Mount Sinai was an "if you do this, then I will do this" kind of agreement.

1. Work your way through the following passages, noting what is said about what God will do based on what the Israelites and their kings do. (This *does not* need to be exhaustive. Just note several key words or phrases for each.)

    a. God speaking to the children of Israel at Mount Sinai through Moses (Lev. 26:1–13)

       If you will . . .

       Then I will . . .

    b. God speaking to the children of Israel at Mount Sinai through Moses (Lev. 26:14–20)

       If you will . . .

Then I will . . .

c. God speaking to Israel as they prepared to enter the Promised
    Land (Deut. 4:25–28)

    If you will . . .

    Then I will . . .

d. God speaking to Israel as they as they prepared to enter the
    Promised Land (Deut. 4:29–31)

    If you will . . .

    Then I will . . .

e. God speaking to Israel as they as they prepared to enter the
    Promised Land (Deut. 28:1–14)

    If you will . . .

    Then I will . . .

f. God speaking to Israel as they as they prepared to enter the
    Promised Land (Deut. 28:15–65; focus on vv. 15–25 and
    63–65)

    If you will . . .

    Then I will . . .

g. Joshua speaking to Israel before his death (Josh. 24:20)

If Israel will . . .

Then God will . . .

h. The Lord speaking to Solomon (1 Kings 9:4–5)

If Solomon will . . .

Then God will . . .

i. The Lord speaking to Solomon (1 Kings 9:6–9)

If Solomon will . . .

Then God will . . .

The twelve tribes of Israel were united under one king during the respective reigns of Saul, David, and Solomon. But after the death of King Solomon, the united kingdom of Israel split into two kingdoms—the southern kingdom of Judah and the northern kingdom of Israel. This means that when we read about "Israel" in the books of 1 Kings and 2 Kings, this does not refer to the entire nation as it has to this point, but only to the kingdom of the northern ten tribes. The northern kingdom of Israel lasted just over two hundred years, led by nineteen kings before they were conquered and taken away into exile by the Assyrian Empire. They never returned to the land and were assimilated into other people groups.

The southern kingdom of Judah lasted slightly over three hundred years, led by nineteen kings, who were all descendants of David, before they too were conquered and taken into exile by the Babylonians. Unlike the northern kingdom, however, a remnant of the southern kingdom was preserved and allowed to return and resettle Jerusalem seventy years later.

2. In 1 Kings 12 we read about Solomon's son Rehoboam, who ascended to the throne after Solomon and determined to increase the already heavy tax burden on the people. This pushed the ten northern tribes to revolt and choose Jeroboam, who was "the son of Nebat, an Ephraimite" to be their king. Read 1 Kings 12:16–20. Why is this choice a problem?

3. Thirty-two times in the books of 1 and 2 Kings we read that a king was "evil in the sight of the Lord." Below are just a few of those kings. Note a few phrases for each, indicating what made these kings and therefore their kingdoms evil.

Jeroboam, king in Israel (1 Kings 12:25–33):

Rehoboam, king in Judah (1 Kings 14:22–23):

Ahab, king in Israel (1 Kings 16:29–33):

Ahaz, king in Judah (2 Kings 16:2–4):

Manasseh, king in Judah (2 Kings 21:1–9):

4. If so many kings were so evil, even in the southern kingdom of Judah, why, according to 2 Kings 8:18–19, did God not just destroy them?

5. Eight times we read in 1 Kings 12—2 Kings 22 that a king was "right in the sight of the LORD." What made these kings right? Note also, for each, what failure or exception is mentioned, lest we think this human king was all that God had promised he would one day set on David's throne.

Asa (1 Kings 15:9–15):

Jehoshaphat (1 Kings 22:41–46):

Hezekiah (2 Kings 18:1–8; 20:12–19):

Josiah (2 Kings 22:1–23:30):

6. At one point in the history of the divided kingdom, a king from the line of David in the south, Jehoram, married the daughter of a king of Israel in the north named Athaliah (2 Kings 8:16–27), and their son Ahaziah later took the throne in Jerusalem. When Ahaziah died, his mother, Athaliah, sought to kill all the descendants of David who might take the throne, and she took the throne herself. This was the only time someone who was not a descendant of David sat on the throne over

Judah during this period. But how, according to 2 Kings 11, did God sovereignly protect the royal line of King David?

7. Read 2 Kings 17:6–18. Why do you think the writer of 2 Kings began his analysis of the fall of the northern kingdom by reminding the reader that the Lord had brought his people out of slavery in Egypt (v. 7)?

8. According to 2 Kings 17:6–18, list at least ten reasons God allowed the northern kingdom to be destroyed and its people exiled.

9. According to 2 Kings 17:13, how had the Lord demonstrated mercy to Israel (and Judah) for centuries?

10. And how had the Israelites responded according to 2 Kings 17:14–18?

11. Joel was a prophet who likely prophesied to Israel before its fall to the Assyrians. Read Joel 2:12–14. What does the prophet say might have happened to Israel had they heeded his warning and repented and returned to the Lord?

12. Briefly summarize what happened to the southern kingdom in 2 Kings 24:10–17.

13. Briefly summarize what happened in 2 Kings 25:8–12.

14. What happened thirty-seven years later according to 2 Kings 25:27–30, and why does this matter?

Teaching Chapter

You Were Warned

My husband has a name for me that he uses on occasion. It is nothing like "Darling" or "Honey" or "Sweetie." It's "Scofflaw," as in one who scoffs at the law. He calls me this when I act as if the rules simply don't apply to me. But aren't some rules made to be broken? Take, for example, the "no outside food or drink" notice at the movie theater. I don't like it, and I have been known to smuggle my can of Diet Coke into the theater and wait for a loud explosion during the previews to cover the sound of opening the can. And before you judge me, you with the big purse, you've done it too, haven't you?

One time we were sitting in a theater and saw some friends of ours come down the opposite aisle and sit down. We watched as she brought out her big bag of microwave popcorn. It was then I realized they weren't just friends; they were fellow scofflaws! So I snuck up behind them and put on my most official-sounding voice and said, "Excuse me, but I'm going to have to ask you to leave." They were very relieved to look up and find it was me nailing them and not the theater manager.

The truth is, I don't think I've ever witnessed this "no outside food or drinks" rule actually being enforced, have you? In fact, I don't think I've ever seen a warning stated clearly about what will happen if we're found sipping on a soda or going for some gummy bears that we didn't purchase from the theater. That is very different from the student handbook that spells out clearly the various infractions that will get you expelled from school, or the youth director's warnings about what pranks will get you sent home from camp. It's also very different from the very clear warnings of the consequences of breaking God's law that were set before the Israelites as they entered into the land of Canaan.

They Were Warned

God began clearly warning the Israelites forty years before they even entered the Promised Land about what would cause them to be evicted from it. In Leviticus we read:

> You shall not do as they do in the land of Egypt, where you lived, and you shall not do as they do in the land of Canaan, to which I am bringing you. . . . Do not make yourselves unclean by any of these things, for by all these the nations I am driving out before you have become unclean, and the land became unclean, so that I punished its iniquity, and the land vomited out its inhabitants. But you shall keep my statutes and my rules and do none of these abominations . . . lest the land vomit you out when you make it unclean, as it vomited out the nation that was before you. (Lev. 18:3, 24–28)

The imagery here is unpleasant, but appropriately so. If you've ever had food poisoning, then you know what your body does to eject the offending poison from your system. This is God's holy land, and the Canaanite people living there have poisoned it with their abominations. It has made God sick to his stomach, and he is about to vomit them out of his land. And as he does so, it should serve as a warning to the Israelites that they can't assume that they can do what the Canaanites did and expect to live forever in his land. They are not an exception to God's rules. They cannot enjoy the blessing of God apart from obedience to God. If they are disobedient, God will judge them just as severely as he judged the nations who contaminated his land before them.

Right before the next generation crossed the Jordan to take possession of the land, Moses warned them again:

> When you father children and children's children, and have grown old in the land, if you act corruptly by making a carved image in the form of anything, and by doing what is evil in the sight of the LORD your God, so as to provoke him to anger, I call heaven and earth to witness against you

today, that you will soon *utterly perish* from the land that you are going over the Jordan to possess. You will not live long in it, but will be *utterly destroyed.* And the LORD will scatter you among the peoples, and you will be left few in number among the nations where the LORD will drive you. (Deut. 4:25–27)

The Israelites entered into the land, but they didn't purge the land of the Canaanites as God had told them to. Their compromise and God's patience continued during the period of the judges. Then the Lord appeared to King Solomon, promising him that if he walked before the Lord, keeping his commands, there would never come a day when one of his descendants would not be on the throne of Israel, but also warning what would happen if he led the people in disobeying and disregarding God's commands:

> But if you turn aside from following me, you or your children, and do not keep my commandments and my statutes that I have set before you, but go and serve other gods and worship them, then I will *cut off* Israel from the land that I have given them, and the house that I have consecrated for my name I will *cast out* of my sight, and Israel will become a proverb and a byword among all peoples. And this house will become a heap of ruins. Everyone passing by it will be astonished and will hiss, and they will say, "Why has the LORD done thus to this land and to this house?" Then they will say, "Because they abandoned the LORD their God who brought their fathers out of the land of Egypt and laid hold on other gods and worshiped them and served them. Therefore the LORD has brought all this disaster on them." (1 Kings 9:6–9)

They heard a promise that David's kingdom would be made sure forever, and perhaps that lulled them into a false sense of security, because they were also told clearly that if they persisted in disobedience to God, they and their king would be swept away into exile. And these warnings were not idle threats.

More than once in my parenting journey I have threatened Matt with punishments that I was sorry I had come up with—punishments that were more miserable for me than for him. And if you promise not to report me to the Parenting Hall of Shame, I will admit to you that more than once I have committed the ultimate parenting faux pas of threatening a punishment I did not follow through on. However, God is a better parent than I am. His rules are always for our good, not for his convenience. And we can be sure that he does not make idle threats. He will always follow through on his promises—including his promises to punish. Of course, usually when we talk about God keeping his promises, we're thinking about his promises to bless. But we should know that God also keeps his promises to curse. All of the punishment he promises, he carries out in full measure. He will not go soft in the end. He will not compromise his justice. It's rather sobering to think about, isn't it? It should be. If you are not sobered by the thought of God measuring out deserved punishment, perhaps you don't really take God all that seriously.

They Were Disobedient

The sad story of the decline and eventual exile of the people of God begins with the words, "The Lord raised up against Solomon an adversary" (1 Kings 11:14). Immediately we realize that this attack is not simply the natural result of forces of history, but something God is doing. Solomon received a kingdom that was united and at peace, but he handed his son a kingdom that was divided and at war. When Rehoboam took over, he immediately faced rumbling discontent among the people in the north, who didn't want him as king. So the northern tribes picked their own king, Jeroboam, who had been one of Solomon's generals but was not a descendant of David, and separated themselves from the tribes of Judah and Benjamin.

Grasp the tragedy here. God had promised to bless people from every nation through a king from the line of David. So when the northern tribes crowned their own king, who was not a son of David, they were separating themselves from the promise and blessing of God. The twelve tribes of Israel had been unified under a great and wise king in the days of Solomon and had enjoyed wealth and peace on every side. They had been the envy of the whole world. But now they were at war with each other.

I have to admit that this part of Israel's history has always been really fuzzy for me. While a childhood filled with learning Bible stories was an incredible blessing, somehow I missed grasping the bigger story that all of those stories fit into. For most of my life, I would have been hard-pressed to summarize the history of Israel from their entrance into the Promised Land and put all of the kings and prophets and exiles and returns in their proper place. When we read through the history found in 1 and 2 Kings, it can be difficult to sort out the chronology of the kings, partly because the narrative goes back and forth between the kings of Israel in the north and the kings of Judah in the south. What makes it even more confusing is that some of the kings have very similar names, and some kings are referred to by more than one name. So if you have trouble putting it all together, I'm with you. But here are the basics we need to understand.

Ten of the twelve tribes became the northern kingdom, which was called Israel, and their capital was in Samaria. The kings who ruled there for about two hundred years were not descendants of David. It is important when reading this section of Bible history that we keep in mind that "Israel" does not refer to the whole nation but just to the ten northern tribes. Two tribes, Judah and Benjamin, became the southern kingdom called "Judah," and its capital was in Jerusalem. Benjamin was a very small tribe and essentially was folded into Judah. For about four hundred years, a descendant of David sat on the throne over Judah.

The first king over the northern ten tribes, Jeroboam, really didn't know or care much about the Lord. But he was savvy enough to recognize the cohesive power of religion as well as the draw of Jerusalem's temple, which was in the heart of the southern kingdom. Jeroboam realized that if his people continued to travel into Judah to worship God at the temple in Jerusalem, they might begin to want back the old unity with the tribes there, and, worse yet, they might want their old davidic king back. So Jeroboam decided to create his own centers of worship for the northern tribes. Rather than building an alternate temple to the one in Jerusalem, he made two golden calves, putting one in the south and one in the north and introduced them to the people, saying, "You have gone up to Jerusalem long enough. Behold your gods, O Israel, who brought you up out of the land of Egypt" (1 Kings 12:28). Thus they wouldn't have to make that long trip to Jerusalem anymore to worship.

Have you ever noticed that often when a company is taking away some service or charging more for it, they send you a letter or an e-mail telling you it is "for your convenience"? That's what Jeroboam is doing here. He is couching his introduction of false worship as a convenience. What they don't realize is how much this "convenience" is going to cost. It's going to cost them everything they hold dear—all the good gifts God has poured out on them in the Land of Promise.

> He also made temples on high places and appointed priests from among all the people, who were not of the Levites. And Jeroboam appointed a feast on the fifteenth day of the eighth month like the feast that was in Judah, and he offered sacrifices on the altar. (1 Kings 12:31–32)

Jeroboam used the same vocabulary, set-up, and yearly calendar for his made-up religion as that of true worship of Yahweh—altars, temples, priests, sacrifices, and feasts. He used all the buzzwords that would make it sound just like the worship of Yahweh, when actually it was a complete rejection of Yahweh.

We get a sense of what life was like in the northern kingdom during these two hundred years from the book of Amos, who was a prophet there during this era. He described it as a place where the rich lived in opulence with total disregard for the poor, and where the streets were filled with violence. In the land where God's people were supposed to be teaching their children the commandments of God and passing along the gracious promises of God, parents were allowing their children to be burned in the fire to false gods.

A tree can be destroyed in two different ways. Either there can be internal rot that does work slowly but surely, or there can be a storm that causes it to snap and blow it down. But when there is both internal rot and the external force of a storm, then a fall is certain. That describes northern kingdom. It was corrupt and rotten inside. And then the powerful storm of the armies of Assyria came up against it, and it was only a matter of time until it fell.[1]

---

[1] This imagery of Israel like a tree experiencing the compounded impact of internal rot and the winds of a storm is adapted from Stuart Olyott's lecture "Promised Land to the Exile: 2 Kings" (Belvidere Road Church, Liverpool, UK, 1979).

They Were Exiled

The Israelites had been warned of what would happen if they lived this way in the land, and God never makes idle threats. So we read in 2 Kings 17:

> Then the king of Assyria invaded all the land and came to Samaria, and for three years he besieged it. In the ninth year of Hoshea, the king of Assyria captured Samaria, and he carried the Israelites away to Assyria and placed them in Halah, and on the Habor, the river of Gozan, and in the cities of the Medes. And this occurred because the people of Israel had sinned against the Lord their God, who had brought them up out of the land of Egypt from under the hand of Pharaoh king of Egypt, and had feared other gods and walked in the customs of the nations whom the Lord drove out before the people of Israel, and in the customs that the kings of Israel had practiced. (2 Kings 17:5–8)

That is the story of the northern kingdom—two hundred years of turning away from Yahweh and going after other gods. And then God did what he said he would do. They were vomited out of the land and into exile in Assyria, scattered throughout Assyria's conquered land. Assyria's method of making sure conquered peoples did not rise up again against them was to move populations from other conquered countries into newly conquered land so that they would intermarry, and any sense of national identity would be obliterated.

> And the king of Assyria brought people from Babylon, Cuthah, Avva, Hamath, and Sepharvaim, and placed them in the cities of Samaria instead of the people of Israel. And they took possession of Samaria and lived in its cities. . . . So these nations feared the Lord and also served their carved images. Their children did likewise, and their children's children— as their fathers did, so they do to this day. (2 Kings 17:24, 41)

When these imported foreigners were brought to Israel, they brought their own gods with them and intermarried with the few Israelites who were left behind on the land. Their descendants were the mixed-race people so hated by Israelites in Jesus's day—the Samaritans. All the rest of the ten northern tribes were eventually assimilated into the lands and the people where they were scattered.

The story in the south was the same but different. Clearly things did not get off to a good start in the southern kingdom.

> Now Rehoboam the son of Solomon reigned in Judah. Rehoboam was forty-one years old when he began to reign, and he reigned seventeen years in Jerusalem, the city that the LORD had chosen out of all the tribes of Israel, to put his name there. His mother's name was Naamah the Ammonite. And Judah did what was evil in the sight of the LORD, and they provoked him to jealousy with their sins that they committed, more than all that their fathers had done. For they also built for themselves high places and pillars and Asherim on every high hill and under every green tree, and there were also male cult prostitutes in the land. They did according to all the abominations of the nations that the LORD drove out before the people of Israel. (1 Kings 14:21–24)

While 1 and 2 Kings says that every one of the nineteen northern kings "did evil in the eyes of the Lord" or "did not turn away from any of the sins" of the previous king, there were a number of kings who reigned in the south who "did what was right in the eyes of the LORD" (2 Kings 15:3). First and 2 Kings commend Asa, Jehoshaphat, Joash, Amaziah, Uzziah, and Jotham. Yet none of them eliminated the places of worship to other gods that had been erected in the days of Solomon. After the northern tribes were exiled, things took a decided turn for the worse in the south when Manasseh came to power. In an ultimate act of defiance against God, Manasseh built altars to pagan gods not just in the hills surrounding the city but *in the temple of the Lord* (2 Kings 21:4–6)! This would be like a wife bringing her lover into her house and sleeping with him right in front of her husband.

We see, however, the grace of God at work preserving this davidic line of kings when Manasseh's grandson Josiah came along. He had grown up in this horrible household of pagan worship, yet he began to seek after the Lord in the temple. There he discovered a manuscript of God's law—probably the book of Deuteronomy—that had been lost. Imagine this: the temple was there, but evidently there had been no reading or teaching of the Scriptures for decades. Josiah then led a national campaign of reformation, making his way around the entire country supervising the destruction of all the altars to idols in the land

(2 Kings 23). But while Josiah had the power to tear down altars, he didn't have the power to change hearts. And soon after his death, the altars to idols were rebuilt, and the false worship resumed. It was during this time that the prophet Jeremiah tried to warn the people of the disaster that was approaching:

> And the LORD says: ". . . They have forsaken my law that I set before them, and have not obeyed my voice or walked in accord with it, but have stubbornly followed their own hearts and have gone after the Baals, as their fathers taught them. Therefore thus says the LORD of hosts, the God of Israel: Behold, I will feed this people with bitter food, and give them poisonous water to drink. I will scatter them among the nations whom neither they nor their fathers have known, and I will send the sword after them, until I have consumed them." (Jer. 9:13–16)

Jeremiah's message of doom began to be fulfilled in 597 BC when Nebuchadnezzar of Babylon captured Jerusalem, desecrated the temple, and deported most of her leaders and artisans.

> At that time the servants of Nebuchadnezzar king of Babylon came up to Jerusalem, and the city was besieged. And Nebuchadnezzar king of Babylon came to the city while his servants were besieging it, and Jehoiachin the king of Judah gave himself up to the king of Babylon, himself and his mother and his servants and his officials and his palace officials. The king of Babylon took him prisoner in the eighth year of his reign and carried off all the treasures of the house of the LORD and the treasures of the king's house, and cut in pieces all the vessels of gold in the temple of the LORD, which Solomon king of Israel had made, as the LORD had foretold. He carried away all Jerusalem and all the officials and all the mighty men of valor, 10,000 captives, and all the craftsmen and the smiths. None remained, except the poorest people of the land. (2 Kings 24:8–14)

Judah was carried off into exile. It didn't have to be this way. They had been warned. They were living under the old covenant, given through Moses at Sinai, an arrangement that God made uniquely with ancient Israel. The old covenant was characterized by conditional promises and severe warnings. God said, "*If* you obey me, *then* I will bless you, and *if* you disobey me, *then* I will curse you" (Deuteronomy 28). The problem wasn't with the covenant but with the people. They just didn't have the want-to to keep up their end of this if-then arrangement.

But God didn't give up on his people. He made a promise of a new covenant to come that would be far superior to the performance-based old covenant. Instead of an if-then relationship, God promised an "I will" relationship through his prophet Jeremiah. He said, "I will put my law within them, and I will write it on their hearts" (Jer. 31:33). God also reaffirmed his earlier promise of a king who would sit on David's throne forever. This king would be righteous, not idolatrous, and under his rule there would be security rather than unrest:

> Behold, the days are coming, declares the LORD, when I will raise up for David a righteous Branch, and he shall reign as king and deal wisely, and shall execute justice and righteousness in the land. In his days Judah will be saved, and Israel will dwell securely. And this is the name by which he will be called: "The LORD is our righteousness." (Jer. 23:5–6)

At the very end of the book, the writer of 2 Kings wants us to see the way God was at work, even during the exile, to bring about this promise of a righteous branch from David.

> And in the thirty-seventh year of the exile of Jehoiachin king of Judah, in the twelfth month, on the twenty-seventh day of the month, Evil-merodach king of Babylon, in the year that he began to reign, graciously freed Jehoiachin king of Judah from prison. And he spoke kindly to him and gave him a seat above the seats of the kings who were with him in Babylon. So Jehoiachin put off his prison garments. And every day of his life he dined regularly at the king's table, and for his allowance, a regular allowance was given him by the king, according to his daily needs, as long as he lived. (2 Kings 25:27–30)

The royal house of David may have been dethroned, imprisoned, and exiled, but it was not obliterated. God always keeps his promises. And because he is a sovereign king, he is powerful enough to preserve for himself the line of King David so that one day David's greater son would be born to sit on David's throne, just as he had promised. Matthew records in his genealogy just how Jesus descended from David, even when his descendants no longer sat on the throne over Judah.

And after the deportation to Babylon: Jechoniah was the father of Shealtiel, and Shealtiel the father of Zerubbabel, and Zerubbabel the father of
Abiud, and Abiud the father of Eliakim, and Eliakim the father of Azor,
and Azor the father of Zadok, and Zadok the father of Achim, and Achim
the father of Eliud, and Eliud the father of Eleazar, and Eleazar the father
of Matthan, and Matthan the father of Jacob, and Jacob the father of Joseph the husband of Mary, of whom Jesus was born, who is called Christ.
(Matt. 1:12–16)

He Was Obedient

Jesus was exiled from God's presence and blessing—but not because of his disobedience.

Matthew makes clear in his Gospel that Jesus was the promised Son of David. He is also intent in his Gospel to demonstrate that Jesus was the true Israel who obeyed God perfectly in a way Israel never could. Just as Israel came out of Egypt, Matthew points out that Jesus came out of Egypt as a child. Just as Israel passed through the waters of the Red Sea, we read about Jesus passing through the waters of baptism. Just as Israel was tempted in the wilderness for forty years, we witness Jesus being tempted in the wilderness for forty days. Jesus went up on the mountain to teach God's law and came down from the mountain to feed the people with bread, like God had fed Israel with the manna in the wilderness. But Jesus's embracing of Israel's story did not end there.

He Was Exiled

Just as Israel was exiled from the place of God's presence and blessing because of her disobedience, so Jesus was exiled from God's presence and blessing—but not because of his disobedience. He was exiled because of *our* disobedience. At the cross, Jesus experienced exile in its most intense form as he was separated from God's blessing. We hear the agony of this exile in Jesus's words from the cross: "My God, my God, why have you forsaken me?" On the cross Jesus experienced the exile from God that you and I deserve to experience forever. He was cut off from God so that we can be welcomed in.

Exile, however, was not the end of the story of Israel, and neither was it the end of the story of Jesus. For Israel, after exile into Babylon came return to the Promised Land. And for Jesus, after exile into death came resurrection to life. Jesus endured the exile of death in order to overcome it. And because he overcame it, all who are joined to him need never fear being eternally exiled from God. "Christ suffered for our sins once for all time. He never sinned, but he died for sinners to bring you safely home to God" (1 Pet. 3:18 NLT).

We've Been Warned

God does not make idle threats. Don't mistake your experience of his mercy as God going soft on sin. All of the punishment he has promised, all of the punishment you rightly deserve, he carries out in full measure. The question is: will it fall on you because you are separated from Christ? Or will you be protected from it because you have hidden yourself in Christ, who has absorbed all the punishment you deserve? The urgency of this question is why Jesus also issued a warning of what will happen to those who refuse to be united to him. He said:

> If anyone does not abide in me he is thrown away like a branch and withers; and the branches are gathered, thrown into the fire, and burned. If you abide in me, and my words abide in you, ask whatever you wish, and it will be done for you. By this my Father is glorified, that you bear much fruit and so prove to be my disciples. (John 15:6–8)

No one who refuses to be joined to Christ and thereby receive his perfect record of obedience as her own can expect to live forever in God's holy land. Instead she can expect to be exiled far away from the place of his blessing. How do we know if we are joined to Christ? Our lives will bear the fruit of obedience to him that comes only from abiding in him. As partakers of the new covenant, our obedience to God is not the way we secure our place in his kingdom. We rest on Christ's obedience for that. Instead, obedience is the natural outflow, or the fruit, of being savingly connected to Christ. Jesus said that if we love him, we will obey him (John 14:23). You see, if you have truly come to Christ, his Spirit is at work in you, revealing areas of disobedience, giving you the desire and the power to forsake sin, and transforming you into a person who wants to obey. This is no self-effort salvation or be-havior modification but a Spirit-empowered transformation.

> *It's not that you obey perfectly, or that you never struggle with sin, but that there is an identifiable pattern of glad obedience to the king taking shape in your life.*

It's not that you obey perfectly, or that you never struggle with sin, but that there is an identifiable pattern of glad obedience to the King taking shape in your life. Instead of produc-ing the kind of fruit that is consistent with a person living her life at odds with the King, resistant to the King, your life is producing the kind of fruit that gives evidence that you have a new desire to obey and a new power to obey. Your connectedness to Jesus means that the things that make God want to vomit, increasingly make you want to vomit. And the things that make God smile are more and more becoming the things that make you smile. Paul wrote in Galatians 5, reiterating the warning Jesus had given:

> Now the works of the flesh are evident: sexual immorality, impurity, sen-suality, idolatry, sorcery, enmity, strife, jealousy, fits of anger, rivalries, dissensions, divisions, envy, drunkenness, orgies, and things like these. I warn you, as I warned you before, that *those who do such things will not inherit the kingdom of God*. But the fruit of the Spirit is love, joy, peace, pa-tience, kindness, goodness, faithfulness, gentleness, self-control; against such things there is no law. And those who belong to Christ Jesus have crucified the flesh with its passions and desires. (Gal. 5:19–24)

When Jesus came, he repeatedly warned that those who persist in living as if God is not their king will be exiled from his kingdom. Any claim to know God that is not expressed in a growing obedience to God cannot be true, saving knowledge of God. So what do we do with these repeated warnings? Are we to live in fear that we won't be obedient enough, that we will somehow cross the line that will make us vulner-able to being cast out of God's heavenly land? The warnings of the New Testament serve to sound the alarm and call those who are not united with Christ to be joined to him so that they will not face the dire fate of being exiled from God forever. They also serve as a means by which we can test the genuineness of our connectedness to Christ. They should cause us to examine ourselves and ask, "Is my life marked by obedience to God?" The question is not, "Am I perfect?" but rather, "Are a desire and determination to be obedient to God shaping my life?"

My friend, don't ignore the warnings found in the Word of God. The way to respond to the warning of God is to respond to the invitation of Christ, which is: "Come to me, all who labor and are heavy laden, and I will give you rest. Take my yoke upon you, and learn from me, for I am gentle and lowly in heart, and you will find rest for your souls. For my yoke is easy, and my burden is light." (Matt. 11:28–30)

In Christ you will find pardon for all of your past disobedience. And connected to Christ, you will find power for living a new life of obedience. He will give you the want-to to obey him so that instead of fearing exile, you will find rest for your soul. He says, "All that the Father gives me will come to me, and whoever comes to me *I will never cast out*" (John 6:38).

Looking Forward

Eternal Exile

The pattern began in the garden of Eden when Adam decided he did not want to live under the rule of God. Adam and Eve broke God's commandment, and they were driven out of the presence of God, exiled from the garden of God. It continued in the Promised Land. In 1 and 2 Kings we find that the people of God living in God's land have turned away from worshiping him and toward living in ways that are an offense to his holiness. God responded to their disobedience in the same way he responded to Adam and Eve's disobedience. The people of God who refused to obey the rule of God were driven out of God's holy land and into exile.

When Christ came, he warned those who would listen that they should expect the same thing in the future—the day is coming when he will send not the armies of Assyria or Babylon, but an army of angels to exile all of those who persist in disobedience:

> The Son of Man will send his angels, and they will gather out of his kingdom all causes of sin and all law-breakers, and throw them into the fiery furnace. In that place there will be weeping and gnashing of teeth. (Matt. 13:41–42)

This will be the ultimate exile from which there will be no opportunity to return, no hopes of returning to feed on. Instead there will be only unending sorrow and regret.

Jesus also had a warning for religious people who were "workers of lawlessness," people who talk the talk of Christianity but have no interest in obeying Christ:

> Not everyone who says to me, "Lord, Lord," will enter the kingdom of heaven, but the one who does the will of my Father who is in heaven. On that day many will say to me, "Lord, Lord, did we not prophesy in your name, and cast out demons in your name, and do many mighty works in your name?" And then will I declare to them, "I never knew you; depart from me, you workers of lawlessness." (Matt. 7:21–23)

Evidently there are many people who are very busy doing things in God's name but are destined not for a home at rest in God's land but for an eternity away from God's presence. Evidently they have presumed upon God's grace and mercy, assuming that they can live a life of lawlessness instead of obedience and that God will overlook it because of their religious activity. My friend, our obedience matters because God's holiness matters.

On that great and terrible day of salvation and judgment when Christ returns, all of those who are joined to Christ and therefore have lived lives seeking to obey him will make their home forever in God's holy land, the new heavens and the new earth. But all of those who have refused to come to Christ for forgiveness and rest and for a new heart and fresh power to walk in his ways will be driven from his presence.

> Blessed are those who wash their robes, so that they may have the right to the tree of life and that they may enter the city by the gates. Outside are the dogs and sorcerers and the sexually immoral and murderers and idolaters, and everyone who loves and practices falsehood. "I, Jesus, have sent my angel to testify to you about these things for the churches. I am the root and the descendant of David, the bright morning star." (Rev. 22:14–16)

Who is offering us this comfort as well as this warning so that we will not be caught unaware and exiled forever? It is Jesus, who is both the one who created David and the Son of David. When the Son of David comes to exercise all of the authority that has been granted to him, we can be sure that he will put an end to all of the disobedience and lawlessness that has infected his land. For those who have come to Christ, this is a promise to be cherished. And for those who refuse to come, it is a warning to be heeded.

Discussion Guide

2 Kings

Getting the Discussion Going

1. Can you relate to Nancy's wishing that she had not come up with some threatened punishments for her son? Or can you think of some warnings you have received that either you are very glad you heeded or you wish you had listened to?

Getting to the Heart of It

2. When we work our way through the warnings recorded in Leviticus and Deuteronomy and elsewhere that led up to the time of the divided kingdom, it seems clear to us what they should and should not have done. Why do you think they did not heed the warnings?

3. Nancy admitted that tracing the history of Israel from the kingdom united under David and Solomon to the divided kingdom, exile, and return from exile has always been fuzzy for her. Can someone or several people summarize this history to help us tighten our grasp of it?

4. Looking back at the Personal Bible Study questions regarding what was evil in the sight of the Lord and what was right in the sight of the Lord, what is offensive to God and what pleases him?

5. Under the old covenant, Israel's experience of blessing came under a conditional "If you will, then I will" arrangement. How is our relationship with God different as partakers of the new covenant?

6. Understanding that Jesus came as the second Adam who obeyed instead of disobeying, and as the true Israel who was faithful to God instead of unfaithful, how did Jesus experience and fulfill even their experience of exile? ~~Hebrew 5:7~~ Mark 15:33 K K

7. This lesson is really sobering to us as we consider the reality of those who refuse to obey God being exiled from him forever. Why should we study this?

|Getting Personal|

8. As you think about the fact that your obedience is not the way you earn a place in God's kingdom but the evidence that you are a citizen of God's kingdom, how do you see the Spirit of God at work in your life, giving you a new desire to do what is "right in God's eyes" and an increasing distaste for what is "evil in the sight of the Lord"? Is there an area or experience you would be willing to share with the group, not in a desire to show off your goodness but to testify to the power of God's grace?

Getting How It Fits into the Big Picture

9. In all the detail of these kings and kingdoms, we see that while there are some kings who do right, none of them always do right, and none of them last on the throne. We might see this as a failure of the monarchy that God established in Israel, but is it? For what purposes might God have sovereignly intended both the establishment and subsequent failure of the kingdom and throne over Israel and Judah?

Ezra and Nehemiah

Personal Bible Study

Ezra and Nehemiah

When we left the story of the people of God in the last lesson, the ten northern tribes had been carried off into exile by the Assyrians and been absorbed in a variety of countries and cultures. The southern tribe of Judah had been carried off into exile into Babylon.

1. Just as the Babylonian invasions began, the prophet Jeremiah prophesied about the coming exile to Babylon. What else did he say would happen, according to Jeremiah 25:1–14 and 29:10?

2. About seventy years after the first exiles were taken to Babylon, King Cyrus of Persia overthrew the Babylonian king. The Jews living in Babylon then became servants to the king of Persia, who had a very different approach to conquered peoples than Babylon. According to Ezra 1:1–4, what did King Cyrus send the people of God living in his kingdom to do?

3. Read Ezra 1:5–11. Why do you think the writer of Ezra provides this detail about what the people took back with them to Jerusalem? What does it say about the true aim of the return and rebuilding?

4. The books of Ezra and Nehemiah were originally one book. They tell the story of three waves of exiles returning to Jerusalem over about a one-hundred-year period of time led by three different leaders with three distinct purposes. The first of these leaders is introduced in Ezra 3. Who is he, what special skill does he employ for what task, and what did he accomplish upon arrival in Jerusalem and then in the second year there?

5. A problem arises in Ezra 4:1–6. What is it?

6. After the work stopped for over twenty years and then started again with encouragement from the prophets Haggai and Zechariah, Ezra 6:16 says that "the people of Israel, the priests and the Levites, and the rest of the returned exiles celebrated the dedication of this house of God with joy." Then what happened for the first time in centuries?

7. In Ezra 7:1–10, we are introduced to the second leader in these books who returned to Jerusalem about sixty years after Zerubbabel with a second wave of returnees from Babylon. Who is it, what role or position did he hold, and what did he set his heart to accomplish?

8. Upon arrival, Ezra discovered and confronted a significant problem in Jerusalem. What was it, according to Ezra 9:1–5?

9. Look back at Ezra 6:21. How does Ezra's description of the makeup of God's people at this point demonstrate that this is not a racial issue but a religious issue? Who were the people of God, according to this verse?

10. Can you think of at least two individuals we've discussed so far in this study of the historical books that are examples of non-Israelites who separated themselves from their people and gods to worship the Lord?

11. In Ezra 9:6–15 how does Ezra refer to the people who are in Jerusalem, and how does he explain their existence?

12. In chapters 9 and 10 we witness Ezra grieving over Israel's sin and calling the people to repentance. Describe the scene depicted in Ezra 10:9–14.

13. Thirteen years after Ezra arrived in Jerusalem, the third leader featured in these two books came to Jerusalem. According to Nehemiah 1:1–2:8, who was he, what was his role or position, and what did he go to Jerusalem to accomplish?

14. What was Nehemiah's invitation to the people of God in Jerusalem (Neh. 2:11–20), and how was it received?

15. Read the taunts of the enemies of God and his people in Nehemiah 4:1–3. How do they remind you of the taunts of another enemy of God's people, Goliath, and how does Nehemiah's response in 4:20 remind you of David's confidence?

16. What is Nehemiah's response when the enemies suggest that he come down from the wall so they can meet (Neh. 6:1–9)?

17. Once the wall was completed, the people gathered in the square, and Ezra read from the Book of the Law of Moses (probably from Deuteronomy). How did they respond, according to Nehemiah 8:5–6?

18. The people wept when they heard God's Word, overcome with a sense of their sinfulness. But Nehemiah did not want them to only weep. What did he invite them to do, in Nehemiah 8:9–12, and why?

19. What did the people do in response to reading the law, according to Nehemiah 8:13–18, and how did they feel about it?

20. What did they do in response to the reading of the Book of the Law, according to Nehemiah 9:1–5?

21. Nehemiah 9:6–38 is a prayer of confession that also serves as a summary of the complete Old Testament history of Israel. Read through this prayer and note five or six statements that describe the goodness of God to Israel throughout its history.

22. According to Ephesians 4:11–13, the people of God are still in the midst of a building project. What is the method and the goal of this building project?

23. According to 1 Peter 2:4–8, God is also still in the midst of a building project. What is he building, and what materials is he using?

Teaching Chapter

So Far Away from God

In 1992, I was in a real crisis. I had left my job at a publishing company to start my own media relations business from home two years before my son Matt was born. I had been intent on showing my clients and media contacts that I could be just as available and accomplish just as much from home as I had done before. I left a job I loved that made me feel important and competent and started working at home, where I felt unimportant and incompetent.

And then I started having health issues. It started with bronchitis that seemed to morph into asthma. But there were other things. In fact, on the day I told David that I thought I might need to go to a podiatrist to deal with some numbness in my toes, he said, "Are you trying to go to every specialist there is within a six-month period of time?" And he was right. I had been to the internist, the ENT, the urologist, the proctologist, the psychologist, the gynecologist, and the pneumologist, and I wasn't getting any better.

But I also knew that my issues weren't just physical. I had grown up in the church, gone to a Christian college, and worked about eight years in Christian publishing at that point. David and I were committed to the hilt at our church. But there was a problem. I was so far away from God. I wasn't talking to him through prayer or listening to him by reading his Word. My great fear was that someone would ask me, "What is God doing in your life right now?" and I would be caught. Of course I would have come up with a good answer, talking about some publishing project I was working on, or some theological topic I was interested in, or some ministry at church I was busy with. But inside I felt like a huge hypocrite, and the weight of it was crushing me.

There had been many times I had come up with some grand plan to discipline myself to read my Bible, but those always fizzled out quickly. It felt like a wall of stony silence and unconfessed sin had built up between God and me, and I didn't know how to break it down or get through it. In fact, I wondered if God would really be interested in taking me back and allowing me to start over—again.

Maybe you know just what I mean. Maybe you're committed to the hilt at church, but you know your heart lingers somewhere far away from God. Or maybe you have avoided the church or left the church, thinking that it is too much trouble, and who needs it anyway? And now you find yourself not only having drifted away from the people who care about the state of your soul, but also having drifted away from the God you once knew. And there is a longing inside you to go home, to find something real with God, to start over with him again.

That's where the people of God were in the books we will look at today. They were far away from the land where God had promised to dwell with them, far away from the temple where they went to find forgiveness for sin, far away from being all that they were meant to be. They were five hundred miles east of Jerusalem in Babylon, in the heart of the world, in an environment designed to assimilate them. The Babylonian regime had brought them far away from home and mixed them with people from other conquered territories and even given them Babylonian names in place of their Hebrew names so that they would leave behind their old lives, their old language, their old ways, and their old God.

But then a new regime came into power. The Persians overtook the Babylonians, and they had a completely different strategy when it came to conquered people and lands. Instead of importing them, they allowed them to live in their own land where they were more likely to be productive and produce tax revenue. Instead of forcing them to accept a new set of gods, they were happy to simply add the god of the conquered people to their own panoply of gods.

This is exactly what we find when we open the book of Ezra, which was once one book with Nehemiah. They really go together to give us the whole story of the return of the exiles. Ezra and Nehemiah tell us the story of the people of God coming home from Babylon to Jerusalem. In several waves, over several decades, a remnant of the people who had left came home to start over—in the land, in the temple, with God—and to be the people that God had always intended for them to be. This story holds out hope to those of us who feel far away from God and want to go home and start over again with him.

He Will Bring His People Home

When we open to Ezra 1 and read about the new regime of Persia, we might think that we're reading about a human strategy at work, but we quickly realize a divine strategy is being carried out by a human king. God is at work to bring his people home.

> In the first year of Cyrus king of Persia, that the word of the LORD by the mouth of Jeremiah might be fulfilled, the LORD stirred up the spirit of Cyrus king of Persia, so that he made a proclamation throughout all his kingdom and also put it in writing: "Thus says Cyrus king of Persia: The LORD, the God of heaven, has given me all the kingdoms of the earth, and he has charged me to build him a house at Jerusalem, which is in Judah. Whoever is among you of all his people, may his God be with him, and let him go up to Jerusalem, which is in Judah, and rebuild the house of the LORD, the God of Israel—he is the God who is in Jerusalem. (Ezra 1:1–3)

What does this mean, "that the word of the LORD by the mouth of Jeremiah might be fulfilled?" Jeremiah was one of those prophets in Judah who had warned his people of the coming judgment of exile if they did not stop their evil ways. And, of course, that is what happened. But Jeremiah also prophesied about what would happen seventy years later:

> This whole land shall become a ruin and a waste, and these nations shall serve the king of Babylon seventy years. Then after seventy years are completed, I will punish the king of Babylon and that nation, the land of the Chaldeans, for their iniquity, declares the LORD. (Jer. 25:11–12)

Later, as they began their exile in Babylon, Jeremiah was with them and reminded them of his earlier word from God:

Thus says the LORD of hosts, the God of Israel, to all the exiles whom I have
sent into exile from Jerusalem to Babylon. . . . When seventy years are
completed for Babylon, I will visit you, and I will fulfill to you my promise
and bring you back to this place. For I know the plans I have for you, declares the LORD, plans for welfare and not for evil, to give you a future and
a hope. Then you will call upon me and come and pray to me, and I will
hear you. You will seek me and find me, when you seek me with all your
heart. I will be found by you, declares the LORD, and I will restore your
fortunes and gather you from all the nations and all the places where I
have driven you, declares the LORD, and I will bring you back to the place
from which I sent you into exile. (Jer. 29:4, 10–14)

> *Going back to
> Jerusalem is not
> just a geographical
> relocation. It is a
> personal transfor-
> mation, a whole-life
> reorientation.*

Ah, now we understand the context of
this oft-quoted and oft-misapplied verse.
This was a specific promise given to a
specific group of people in a specific historical situation. What did God's plans for
them include, and why would he need to
assure them that his plans were for good?
His plans included many more years of
exile before the people would get to go
home to Jerusalem. The years of enslavement ahead of them would certainly not seem like "plans for welfare and not for evil." So we see that
this is not a promise that the plans God has for the years of our lives
on earth are going to fit our description of good. They may not be at
all what we are hoping for. In fact, the people of God in Jeremiah's day
were in exile for seventy years. Seventy years is a lifetime. We might
have a lifetime of not getting the things we hope for in the here and
now of this world.

The future and hope that God was setting before them, and that he
sets before you and me, is that that when we seek him, he will be find-
able. Notice from Jeremiah's prophecy the sense of what it is going to
mean to go back to Jerusalem. Going back to Jerusalem means calling
upon the Lord, coming to him, praying to him, seeking him, and finding
him. Going back to Jerusalem is not just a geographical relocation. It is
a personal transformation, a whole-life reorientation—away from the

world that wants to assimilate them and toward the city of God where God wants to sanctify them to himself.

> Then rose up the heads of the fathers' houses of Judah and Benjamin, and the priests and the Levites, everyone whose spirit God had stirred to go up to rebuild the house of the LORD that is in Jerusalem. (Ezra 1:5)

So those exiles who were most zealous to return from Babylon to Jerusalem, those in whom God had stirred up a burning desire to worship God in the place God had promised to dwell, headed home. Chapter 2 of Ezra begins: "Now these were the people of the province who came up out of the captivity of those exiles whom Nebuchadnezzar the king of Babylon had carried captive to Babylonia" (v. 1). And if you're like most people, you think, *This is a chapter of the Bible I'm going to skip. Who needs to read all of these unpronounceable names? Why is this even in the Bible?*

It's here so we will know that these families going back to Jerusalem are the descendants of Abraham, the ones to whom God gave the promise of the land. These are the same families who had left the land, the ones to whom God had made the promise that he would bring them back. But beyond the Israelite exiles who were returning to the land, the list includes others who were not descendants of Abraham who had joined themselves to God's people and wanted in on the promises of God. Ezra 6 describes those who celebrated the first Passover in the land, saying that "it was eaten by the people of Israel who had returned from exile, and also by every one who had joined them and separated himself from the uncleanness of the peoples of the land to worship the LORD, the God of Israel" (Ezra 6:21). We've seen that just as there were Egyptians who joined God's people when they walked out of Egypt, and Canaanites and Moabites such as Rahab and Ruth who became a part of God's people by forsaking their false gods and worshiping Yahweh alone, we see now that God is adding to the list of his people many from throughout the lands conquered by the Persians. God has always been and always will be about the work of bringing people from every tribe and tongue and nation to himself.

But there is something else we should see in this list, which we might be tempted to skip over. We should see that God's people are not nameless, faceless people to him. God likes to keep lists of those who are his people, because his people as a group matter to him, his people as families matter to him, and his people as individuals matter to him.

This list of people in Ezra 2 is actually just the first wave of people who left Babylon to go to Jerusalem to rebuild the temple. We read in chapter 8 of Ezra about a second wave of people coming home from Babylon to Jerusalem. Eventually about fifty thousand people returned, really a very small remnant of the estimated two million exiles who continued to live away from the land and were eventually assimilated into those people groups. The lists of God's people in Ezra and Nehemiah represent the people who were willing to leave Babylon and its familiarity and comforts to go home to the land where God had promised to dwell with them. To go from Babylon to Jerusalem is to go from being scattered to gathered, from alienated to accepted, from outcast to favored child. Is God stirring in your heart to come home from Babylon to Jerusalem, from far away from him to at home with him?

He Will Call His People to Worship

The temple was a tangible demonstration of God dwelling in the midst of his people, and it had been destroyed. For seventy years there had been no sacrifices offered for sin, no priests carrying their concerns into God's presence, no blood being sprinkled, no incense being burned, no lamps being lit, no bread being placed and replaced on the table. And because of this there had been no remedy for the remission of sin, no way for atonement to be made and the peace of promised forgiveness to be found. When God's people headed back to Jerusalem, they were sure to bring priests and Levites and singers with them. They took all of the utensils that Nebuchadnezzar had stripped from the temple of Jerusalem and placed in the temple to his gods. And the first thing they did when they got to Jerusalem was to build an altar to offer sacrifices. Under the leadership of Zerubbabel they began laying the foundation for rebuilding the temple. Clearly the priority of those returning to Jerusalem was to restore the worship of God. The people of God were not merely going home to a land but to the place where they had known and related to God.

It was only a short time after they starting building the foundation for the temple that the opposition began. There is always opposition to genuine worship. The people who had moved into and around Jerusalem during the exile criticized and intimidated the returnees and frustrated their plans so that it took twenty years for the temple to be rebuilt and for temple worship to be restored. But finally the glad day came.

> The people of Israel, the priests and the Levites, and the rest of the returned exiles, celebrated the dedication of this house of God with joy. They offered at the dedication of this house of God 100 bulls, 200 rams, 400 lambs, and as a sin offering for all Israel 12 male goats, according to the number of the tribes of Israel. And they set the priests in their divisions and the Levites in their divisions, for the service of God at Jerusalem, as it is written in the Book of Moses. (Ezra 6:16–19)

He Will Build His City

When the book of Nehemiah opens, it takes our focus back to the place where hundreds of thousands of exiles were still living, including a man named Nehemiah, who had risen to the trusted position of cupbearer to the king of Persia. But evidently, though Nehemiah's whole life had been spent in Babylon, his heart was firmly planted in Jerusalem. One of his brothers who had been to Jerusalem came to see him, and Nehemiah wanted to know how those who had gone back and rebuilt the temple were doing.

> And they said to me, "The remnant there in the province who had survived the exile is in great trouble and shame. The wall of Jerusalem is broken down, and its gates are destroyed by fire." (Neh. 1:3)

Nehemiah couldn't just say, "Well, that's too bad," and go back to his wine tasting. These were his people. This was the city of his God. Nehemiah records:

> As soon as I heard these words I sat down and wept and mourned for days, and I continued fasting and praying before the God of heaven. (Neh. 1:4)

The temple had been rebuilt, but without the wall, the city was still virtually defenseless. These were the walls around the place where God had promised to bring forth his forever rule, and they were in ruin. The reality of it pierced Nehemiah to the core. Nehemiah was allowed to return to Jerusalem with the blessing of the king. And when he arrived, he discovered that even the grim description his brother had given him did not fully capture the reality of the ruined city. Jerusalem was a fallen and charred heap of rubble. Giant stones that had once been embedded in the city's great wall lay half buried and embedded in the earth, and the grass had grown tall around them. The mortar that had once held those stones together was now only dust kicked up by his horse's hooves. By the light of the moon, Nehemiah surveyed the once-glorious city. But Nehemiah saw it all through the lens of the promises of God. He looked at the stones and saw them as a picture of the people of God—broken down, needing to be reclaimed and restored. So he gathered the priests, the nobles, the officials, and those who were to do the work and said:

> "You see the trouble we are in, how Jerusalem lies in ruins with its gates burned. Come, let us build the wall of Jerusalem, that we may no longer suffer derision." And I told them of the hand of my God that had been upon me for good, and also of the words that the king had spoken to me. And they said, "Let us rise up and build." So they strengthened their hands for the good work. (Neh. 2:16–18)

"All God's people gave themselves to the one thing—the rebuilding of the wall—that the greatness and grandeur and glory of God might have visible place again."[1] But no great work for God is done without its detractors, without facing opposition. Remember that ever since the garden of Eden, the seed of the Serpent has been set against the seed of the woman, seeking to defeat the purposes of God in the world. Sanballat and Tobiah, governors over the area surrounding Jerusalem, were displeased that someone had come to help the people of Israel. So they hindered the rebuilding of the wall at every turn. Nehemiah heard his detractors saying, "Do they actually think they can make something of stones from a rubbish heap—and charred ones at that?" (Neh. 4:2 NLT).

---

[1] David Helm, "Nehemiah," sermon (Holy Trinity Church, Chicago, September 17, 2006).

They sent messengers to Nehemiah when he was working on the wall, asking him to come and meet with them. But Nehemiah sent messengers back to them, saying, "I am doing a great work and I cannot come down" (Neh. 6:3).

> So the wall was finished on the twenty-fifth day of the month Elul, in fifty-two days. And when all our enemies heard of it, all the nations around us were afraid and fell greatly in their own esteem, for they perceived that this work had been accomplished with the help of our God. (Neh. 6:15–16)

Fifty-two days. No cranes. No cement trucks. Everyone was made part of the work crew. It was clear not only to God's people but to all of the surrounding peoples and nations who were watching that God had brought his people home, and he was at work in them and through them.

He Will Speak to His People through His Word

God had called his people to worship. He built and secured a city for them, a place where he could dwell with them. And now he wanted to speak to them through his Word.

> And all the people gathered as one man into the square before the Water Gate. And they told Ezra the scribe to bring the Book of the Law of Moses that the LORD had commanded Israel. (Neh. 8:1)

Ezra, from the priestly line of Aaron, was a scribe skilled in the law of Moses. We can almost hear the people begin to chant for Ezra to bring out the book and begin to teach. They're saying, "Bring out the book! Bring out the book!"

> And all the people gathered as one man into the square before the Water Gate. And they told Ezra the scribe to bring the Book of the Law of Moses that the LORD had commanded Israel. And he read from it facing the square before the Water Gate from early morning until midday, in the presence of the men and the women and those who could understand. And the ears of all the people were attentive to the Book of the Law. (Neh. 8:1, 3)

Get the picture of what is happening here. All the people—all the men and women and children who are old enough to understand—have gathered to listen to Ezra read to them from Genesis and Exodus and Leviticus and Numbers and Deuteronomy. From dawn until about noon they listened to Ezra read, and twelve Levites moved among the crowd explaining what Ezra had read, helping them to grasp the story of the curse in Genesis 3 and the promise of a seed of the woman, the promise made to Abraham, and his coming to the very place they were gathered, to offer his son Isaac. The Levites went out into the crowd helping them to understand the substitutionary sacrifices prescribed in Leviticus and the call in Deuteronomy to love the Lord with all of their heart, soul, and might. They taught them about God's deliverance of his people from Egypt and through the Red Sea, about how he gave them the land as an inheritance and came down to live in their midst in the Most Holy Place. And how did they respond?

> And all the people answered, "Amen, Amen," lifting up their hands. And they bowed their heads and worshiped the Lord with their faces to the ground. (Neh. 8:6)

Recently I was speaking at a women's conference, and before I got up to speak, a woman got up and recited the entire book of Colossians. But it wasn't really reciting. It was more like she became Paul and communicated the letter of Colossians. And when she was finished, the room erupted in applause. And if I had had the courage to do what I felt in my heart was the most appropriate thing to do, I would have fallen with my face to the ground in wonder and worship and submission— just from hearing God's Word. It has such power and authority. But I was too reserved, too concerned with how awkward it might be.

The Bible is not just dry history or the description of a religious system or a series of rules for living. It is God condescending to speak to us in human language. And when the voice of the living God speaks, and we understand what he is saying, it blesses us and breaks us and brings us to our knees, sometimes even prostrate before him. At least, it should. Oh, the joy of being undone by hearing the Word of God and having it penetrate deep into our soul!

Hearing God speak to them brought them to tears. It also strengthened them with the joy of the Lord so that they celebrated. It confronted them with their sin and called them to confession. But being confronted with their sin led to more than just confession. It called them to action.

He Will Set His People Apart from the World

As they listened to the Word of God, they heard God's repeated commands to devote the Canaanites to destruction so that they would not intermarry with them and begin to worship their gods. They put that together with their own history of intermarriage and idolatry that had forced them into exile.

> The people of Israel were assembled with fasting and in sackcloth, and with earth on their heads. And the Israelites *separated themselves* from all foreigners and stood and confessed their sins and the iniquities of their fathers. (Neh. 9:1–2)

This is a picture of costly obedience, of a rigorous response to God's command to be holy, set apart. This can appear to us as ungodly—to divorce and send away foreign wives. And it can also be a bit confusing, because we know that some foreign wives had been gladly welcomed in, such as a Canaanite prostitute named Rahab and a Moabite named Ruth. What we must understand is that this commanded separation was not a racial issue; it was a religious issue. The people of Ezra and Nehemiah's day are not being asked to separate themselves from foreign wives who have forsaken their false gods and embraced the promises of the one true God. They are separating themselves from foreign wives who have not forsaken their false gods but have brought their gods—with their carved idols and deviant sexual practices—into their marriages to be mixed with the worship of the one true God.

To come home from Babylon to Jerusalem meant turning their back on the world and its idolatrous ways to worship and serve God alone. For them, and for us, this requires rigorous self-examination, identifying and eliminating anything and everything that wants to woo us away from our worship of God alone.

When we come to the end of the book of Nehemiah, we're essentially at the end of Israel's Old Testament history. Yes, there are plenty of books that follow Nehemiah in our Bibles, but they are the wisdom books and the prophetical books, which were written mostly during the time covered in the history books. After Nehemiah, there is no further biblical record of Israel's history until the story picks up again with the visit of an angel to a priest named Zechariah, who will become the father of John the Baptist.

Here at the end of the book of Nehemiah, we learn that Nehemiah had to live up to his commitment to go back to King Cyrus. So he was gone from Jerusalem for a while after the wall was rebuilt. In Nehemiah 13 we read about Nehemiah's return to Jerusalem about a decade later. When he got there, he found that an Ammonite, Tobiah, who worshiped a false God, not Yahweh, had been given a place to work in the temple. He found that the people were not giving their offerings so that the Levites were forced to work in the fields to be able to eat. The people were treating the Sabbath like any other day of doing business. Nehemiah found that, sadly, once again, Jews had married women from the nations around them. In fact, as he walked through the city he discovered that instead of speaking the language of Judah, the children were speaking the languages of their foreign mothers.

Jesus has thrown open the doors of the city of God and invited all who will turn their back on the Babylons of this world to come in.

Nehemiah's book ends with the prayer of his heart: "Remember me, O my God, for good" (Neh. 13:31). There's a sense of hopelessness and resignation to it. He has tried. He has done everything he knew to do to protect and preserve and purify God's people. And it just wasn't enough. The temple Zerubbabel had rebuilt was not enough to call the people to the kind of worship God is worthy of. Ezra's teaching wasn't enough to keep them confessing their sin and celebrating God's goodness. And the wall Nehemiah built could not keep out the compromise that was continually contaminating God's people.

Let's face it. It's been clear ever since that dark day in the garden. We are ruined by sin and in need of a restorer greater than Nehemiah. Like Nehemiah, we need one who has a heart that is broken over the broken-down state of the people God loves and the place in which he intends to dwell. And that is the restorer God has sent to us. Jesus left the palace of heaven and came to us so that he might reclaim us from the wreckage. He came to call us to true worship, not by reinstating the burnt offerings in the temple but by offering himself as the once-for-all sacrifice. Jesus, the living word, came to teach us what it means to obey God's commands. Jesus has thrown open the doors of the city of God and invited all who will turn their back on the Babylons of this world to come in.

Jesus came on a building project to build his church—a church built not on a foundation of stone but on the foundation of the rock-solid reality that he is the Christ, the son of the living God (Matt. 16:16). Christ is building his church not by climbing up on a wall in Jerusalem to work but by being lifted up on a cross outside Jerusalem, where he accomplished his greatest work, a work that faced great opposition.

> Those who passed by derided him, wagging their heads and saying, "Aha! You who would destroy the temple and rebuild it in three days, save yourself, and come down from the cross!" So also the chief priests with the scribes mocked him to one another, saying, "He saved others; he cannot save himself. Let the Christ, the King of Israel, come down now from the cross that we may see and believe." Those who were crucified with him also reviled him. (Mark 15:29–32)

Those who opposed Christ's work called for him to come down. But Jesus did not come down. We can almost hear him saying the words of Nehemiah: "I am doing a great work and I cannot come down!" (Neh. 6:3). And because he stayed there, accomplishing his redeeming work until he cried out, "It is finished!," you and I can live safely inside the walls of his city where no enemy will be able to bring us harm.

Jesus said, "I will build my church, and the gates of hell shall not prevail against it." (Matt. 16:17). He is building his church—not with fresh-cut stones but with charred and ruined stones—a church made up of people who have been ruined and scarred by sin. Joined by faith to him, we are transformed into living stones and built into a spiritual temple and a city in which God condescends to dwell by his Spirit.

Years ago, when I was so far away from God, not sure how to get home or if I'd be welcomed in, God brought me home to himself. It required leaving where I was in the world with its priorities and perspective. I had to head full-out in his direction to go where I could hear him speak to me through his Word. I joined a Bible study that required rigorous accountability and work on my part. And as I studied his Word, I heard his voice. I came under conviction, and I repented and took steps of costly obedience. And as the months and then years went by, God built a new foundation in my life that was solid. He renewed and rebuilt me. The time came when I realized that I didn't live in fear of being exposed as a hypocrite anymore. I knew he was at work in me—teaching me, changing me, using me. He is still at work in me, making me into a person in whom he delights to dwell by his Spirit.

If you find yourself far away from God, won't you set out today to come home? Don't wait any longer. You will not find an impenetrable wall, but open arms. He is not looking for perfect people who show no signs of being burned by this world. He takes ruined stones and builds them into the kind of place in which he intends to dwell forever.

Looking Forward

The New Jerusalem

At the end of human history, all of those who have overcome the allure of the Babylons of this world and have set their face toward the city of God will enter into that great city.

> And he carried me away in the Spirit to a great, high mountain, and showed me the holy city Jerusalem coming down out of heaven from God, having the glory of God, its radiance like a most rare jewel, like a jasper, clear as crystal. It had a great, high wall, with twelve gates, and at the gates twelve angels, and on the gates the names of the twelve tribes of the sons of Israel were inscribed—on the east three gates, on the north three gates, on the south three gates, and on the west three gates. And the wall of the city had twelve foundations, and on them were the twelve names of the twelve apostles of the Lamb. (Rev. 21:10–14)

For the full significance of the New Jerusalem to sink in, we have to think for a minute about the Old Jerusalem. Jerusalem was the city that David captured from the pagan Jebusites and then dishonored with adultery and murder. This was the city that became infamous for its child sacrifices and unlawful sorceries in the era of the divided kingdom. This was the city that mocked the saintly integrity of Jeremiah and turned a deaf ear to the powerful preaching of Isaiah before the exile. This city was twice destroyed in judgment, first by the God-directed armies of Babylon and later by the Christ-prophesied Roman soldiers under Titus. Jerusalem is the city that rejected and crucified Jesus.

Isn't this the most unlikely of cities to serve as a model for heaven? What does this tell us about heaven? It tells us that God is making a holy city out of our idol-loving, God-defying, Christ-rejecting city of man. God is taking people who worship idols of pleasure and pride, people who love to hate God, and people who continually reject the riches of Christ for the trinkets of the world, and he is remaking us into a city he wants to live in forever. This new city is none other than the church—the church made up not of perfect people but of forgiven sinners.

Revelation tells us about the gates and foundation of the New Jerusalem that John saw.

> It had a great, high wall, with twelve gates, and at the gates twelve angels, and on the gates the names of the twelve tribes of the sons of Israel were inscribed—on the east three gates, on the north three gates, on the south three gates, and on the west three gates. And the wall of the city had twelve foundations, and on them were the twelve names of the twelve apostles of the Lamb. (Rev. 21:12–14)

Among the twelve sons of Jacob and the twelve apostles we find some colossal sinners—adulterers, murderers, thieves—people who, at times, wanted nothing to do with God and lived only for themselves. So the city of God is built on the foundation of the grace of God at work in the lives of ordinary, fearful, unfaithful, inconsistent people who have come to Christ, asking him to do what only he can do—make them clean and new and usable in his kingdom.

Do you see the beauty in this? This means that there is nothing so evil or irredeemable in our lives, nothing so unworthy about our lives, that cannot, even now, be fashioned into the foundation stones of the city of heaven. All of those who set their face to go to the New Jerusalem by joining themselves to Christ will one day be welcomed in.

Discussion Guide

Ezra and Nehemiah

Getting the Discussion Going

1. Interestingly, the three key leaders in Ezra and Nehemiah—Zerubbabel, who led in the rebuilding of the temple; Ezra, who taught the Word; and Nehemiah, who rebuilt the wall—are not the typical prophets, priests, kings, patriarchs, or judges we see throughout the Old Testament. They are a building project manager, a lay teacher, and a civil servant. Can you think of some people you know who are not pastors or church staff members whom you have seen God use in incredible ways to build up his church?

Getting to the Heart of It

2. Try to put yourselves in the place of the exiles living in Babylon. In what ways or for what reasons would you be tempted to just adapt and assimilate? What hopes or promises would encourage you to persevere in holiness?

3. In Ezra we read that "everyone whose spirit God had stirred to go" went back to Jerusalem to build the temple. God stirred them, and what was their part? How is this a picture of God's part and our part in returning to him?

predestination

4. What does it say about these returning exiles, that the first thing they gave themselves to was rebuilding the temple? What do you think they would have looked forward to in having the rebuilt temple?

5. The entire chapter of Nehemiah 9 is a confession of sin. Why is confession of sin a good thing? Should it be public or private? First John says to confess our sins to each other. What good does that do?

6. Throughout our study of the Old Testament we've seen God's repeated displeasure over his people intermarrying with those around them. Does this make God a racist? Why or why not? And does this have any significance for us today? (See 2 Cor. 6:14–18)

7. Oftentimes when we hear the book of Nehemiah taught, it is all about looking at Nehemiah as an example of sound leadership. And he was an effective leader. But Jesus said that the whole of the Old Testament is about Jesus himself. On the road to Emmaus, when Jesus started at the beginning of the Old Testament and explained "to them in all the Scriptures the things concerning himself," (Luke 24:27), what do you think he might have said about the books of Ezra and Nehemiah? In what ways are these books about him?

Getting Personal

8. Perhaps some of us have had the experience Nancy described of finding herself very far away from God and wondering if she would be welcomed back in. Have you? And if so, how did a return to worship, hearing God's Word, and responding to God's Word in repentance and fresh obedience play a role in your coming home?

Getting How It Fits into the Big Picture

9. This is another one of those stories in the Old Testament that we want to end with a happily-ever-after ending, and it doesn't. Nehemiah was gone for a while, and the people went back to their sinful disobedience. How does this actually point us to and prepare us for Christ?

Week 10

Esther

Personal Bible Study

Esther

While the book of Esther falls in the Bible after the books of Ezra and Nehemiah, the story related in the book takes place right in the middle of the events described in Ezra and Nehemiah. It takes place between the first wave of Jews making their way back to Jerusalem to rebuild the temple and Ezra's leading the second return of a group of Jewish exiles to Jerusalem. The first king over the Persian Empire, Cyrus, had released Jews to go back to Jerusalem. When Darius ascended to the throne of Persia, he affirmed the earlier decree of Cyrus and encouraged the continuation of the work. The story of Esther takes place during the reign of the next king, Xerxes (also called Ahasuerus), and before Artaxerxes, the king to whom Nehemiah was a cupbearer.

1. Read Esther 1, which introduces us to the human king ruling over God's people in those days. What sense do you get about this king in regard to what is important to him and how he uses his authority?

2. Read Esther 2:1–7, which introduces us to Mordecai and Esther. List some details we learn in these verses about each of them.

3. Read Esther 2:8–18 and think through the realities of what is happening here. Each of these young women is going to spend one night with the king, and those whom he doesn't choose to be his queen will spend the rest of their lives living in the harem, never having a family but kept in comfort. The text doesn't overtly reveal how Esther feels about this, whether she sees it as a great loss of her plans for her life or as a great opportunity. We do see her responding to the test of serving a foreign king very differently from how another young Jew did. Read Daniel 1:1–21 and 3:8–18 and note similarities and differences between Daniel's experience in the pagan king's palace and Esther's experience in the pagan king's palace.

Similarities:

Differences:

4. Read Esther 2:19–23 and summarize in a sentence or two what happened.

5. In chapter 3 we are introduced to the king's right-hand man, Haman, and told that he is "the Agagite." This doesn't mean much to us, but it would have to the Jews living in Susa who knew their Jewish history. Read Exodus 17:8–16; 1 Samuel 15:1–33; and Esther 3:1–6. How might the history shown here explain what motivates both Mordecai and Haman's attitudes and actions? (Remember from 2:5 that Mordecai, like King Saul, was a descendant of Kish.)

6. Describe in a sentence or two what happens in Esther 3:7–15.

7. Read Esther 4. What does Mordecai want Esther to do, and how does he seek to motivate her to do it (vv. 12–14)?

8. Read Esther 5:1–8. What does Esther now have the king on record as saying, as she works up to asking that her life and that of her people be spared?

9. Read Esther 5:9–14. Note the advice given to Haman by his wife and friends.

10. Read Esther 6. Esther is one of those books that never mentions God. But how do you see God at work in hidden ways in this chapter?

11. Describe in a sentence or two what happens in Esther 7.

12. Haman is dead, but that does not deal with the edict broadcast throughout the kingdom that the Jews are to be killed, an edict that cannot be revoked or retracted. What plan did Mordecai come up with to deal with this edict, and how did it work out, according to Esther 8:9–9:7?

Teaching Chapter

Tale of Two Kingdoms

I spent a lot of years as a publicist representing to the media various Christian authors and organizations. And I suppose it was somewhat obvious that I was in that role because I was a Christian myself. But there was also a sense in which I maintained a professional distance from whatever message it was that my client was communicating as I worked with various media people, many of whom were not believers. But then came the day when I was the author, and I was the one sitting in a restaurant being interviewed about what I believed by a writer from a major newspaper. And it was different. It was like I was crossing over a threshold, going public with my faith in Christ in a new and dramatic way. And, honestly, I wasn't sure I wanted to. It felt a little bit like I had walked out on the plank of a pirate ship and was about to be forced to jump into shark-infested waters. I knew it might cost me.

When the article with the interview was published, it read, in part:

> Guthrie says: No heaven without Jesus. Anyone who doesn't stand on a relationship with God through his son—regardless of their religious or spiritual label—is shut out. It's a tough call in a society where most Americans, polls say, see many paths to God. "I know that sounds exclusive and narrow and intolerant and perhaps even simple-minded to some," Guthrie writes. "But . . . it's the truth. And if you have missed reckoning with Jesus . . . you've missed the very purpose for which you were created."[1]

---

[1] Cathy Lynn Grossman, "Mother Faces God through Grief," *USA Today*, July 16, 2002.

After the article appeared, David came across a response to it online that described me as "decent" but my theology as "poor and damaging." The writer said: "At the heart of the tragic incomprehension among many Christians is the assertion that the only hope for us all is in Jesus." So while it felt like a significant step to go public with my allegiance to Christ in this way, if the worst persecution I've experienced is being described as "decent," my big, brave stand hasn't really cost me very much.

Today, as we bring our study of the historical books to a close, we're looking at the story of Esther, a woman whose identification with the people of God could have cost her everything. She had to decide if she was going to be defined by her citizenship in the kingdom of this world, which promised her a life of comfort, or if she was going to be defined by her citizenship in the kingdom of God, which would threaten her very existence. She faced a choice that all of us face. The day will come when we have to decide what is going to define us. Are we going to be defined by the things of this world—what we can accomplish, how good we can look, the comfort we can enjoy, the status we can attain? Or will we be defined by our belonging to the people of God, as one whose life isn't really about us at all but about the one to whom we've been united by faith?

Celebration in the Kingdom of the World

The book of Esther begins with a party. And this is not just any party. This is a six-month-long party thrown by King Ahasuerus for all of the warlords and governors from throughout his kingdom, which stretched from India to Ethiopia. When we read about the party, we're meant to be impressed by the décor, the furniture, the mosaic tiles, the wine, and even the wine goblets. But I think, perhaps, we're meant to be somewhat amused by the king himself.

> On the seventh day, when the heart of the king was merry with wine, he commanded Mehuman, Biztha, Harbona, Bigtha and Abagtha, Zethar and Carkas, the seven eunuchs who served in the presence of King Ahasuerus, to bring Queen Vashti before the king with her royal crown, in order to show the peoples and the princes her beauty, for she was lovely to look at. But Queen Vashti refused to come at the king's command delivered

by the eunuchs. At this the king became enraged, and his anger burned within him. (Est. 1:10–12)

Here is the most powerful man in the world, and he can't get his queen to come in and prove to his dinner companions that he is married to the most beautiful woman in the world. Of course, they've been drinking for a while now, probably trading stories and one-upping each other. And perhaps the stories are getting more and more bawdy. Perhaps when he asks her to come in with her royal crown, he's really asking for Vashti to come wearing *only* her royal crown. Whatever the reason for it, her refusal creates an embarrassing dilemma for the king, and it is the first of many times throughout the book of Esther that the king asks his advisors what to do. He is supposedly the one with all the power, but evidently it is his advisors who pull the strings. They're afraid that all of the women in the kingdom will hear about Vashti's refusal of her husband's request and will be empowered to refuse the requests of their own husbands. So what is their brilliant advice? Publish throughout the kingdom that Vashti is banished and that every man should be master in his own house.

Now, I no longer have a media relations business, but I'm thinking that if the king had wanted to save face, maybe it wasn't the best idea to make sure that the news about what Vashti had done was published in every corner of the kingdom. But they didn't ask me. So Vashti is out, and there is an opening in the kingdom for the position of queen. And once again the king's advisors have a great idea about how to fill the position.

Then the king's young men who attended him said, "Let beautiful young virgins be sought out for the king. And let the king appoint officers in all the provinces of his kingdom to gather all the beautiful young virgins to the harem in Susa the citadel, under custody of Hegai, the king's eunuch, who is in charge of the women. Let their cosmetics be given them. And let the young woman who pleases the king be queen instead of Vashti." This pleased the king, and he did so. (Est. 2:2–4)

This is like a casting call for *The Bachelor: Susa Edition.* Beautiful young women are going to live together in the same house at the palace complex and compete to be chosen by the king after an overnight date.

Assimilation in the Kingdom of the World

It is at this point that we are introduced to Hadassah, which is her Jewish name, or Esther, which is her Persian name (Est. 2:7). Perhaps we're given both names because the writer is hinting to us that the day is going to come when Esther is going to have to choose which of these two identities will define her. Esther is an exile living in the kingdom of Persia about fifty years after King Cyrus had conquered the Babylonians. So what takes place in the book of Esther actually falls within the time period we were in last week—the time after Zerubbabel took back the first group of exiles to rebuild the temple in Jerusalem, which we read about in Ezra, and the time before Nehemiah led the third wave of exiles to return to rebuild the walls of Jerusalem. And this fact alone tells us something about Esther and her cousin Mordecai. It has been fifty years since the Jews living throughout the provinces ruled by the Persian king have been free to return to Judah. And evidently Mordecai and Esther don't want to. Evidently they just don't have the desire or the drive to live in the land where Yahweh has promised to dwell with his people. Instead they are content to continue to call this kingdom home, where the watchword of the day is *assimilation*, a place where everyone is invited to bring his or her own god to the table, an environment in which the suggestion that there is only one true God is soundly rejected. And evidently they have settled into a comfortable coexistence.

Esther was quite beautiful, which did not escape the eyes of the king's officers, so she was taken to the palace to begin treatments to make her even more beautiful for the king. There at the palace she "was winning favor in the eyes of all who saw her" (Est. 2:15). It is interesting that the writer says that she was "winning" favor, which is different from the account of Daniel, who was in a similar position as a Jew in the palace of Babylon a hundred years earlier. The book of Daniel says that God gave Daniel favor. Evidently Esther was working for it. "Resistance was not high on her program at this point; on the contrary, she seemed content, even eager to be assimilated."[2]

---

[2] Ian Duguid, *Esther and Ruth*, Reformed Expository Commentary, ed. Philip G. Ryken and Richard D. Phillips (Phillipsburg, NJ: P&R, 2005), 23.

> Esther had not made known her people or kindred, for Mordecai had com-
> manded her not to make it known. (Est. 2:10)

The writer of the book of Esther doesn't tell us what Mordecai's reasons were for counseling Esther to hide that she was a Jew. Most likely
he knew that it would not work for her but could likely work against
her. Perhaps Mordecai is trying to protect her, or maybe he's just trying
to give her more chance for advancement. Esther does seem intent on
making an impression at the palace. After a year of filling out her curves
by eating the king's food and getting every treatment offered at the Palace Beauty Salon, she had her one-night tryout with the king. Unlike the
modern version of *The Bachelor*, if you weren't chosen by this bachelor,
you couldn't leave and find another husband. Instead, you were moved
into the concubine part of the house. You would never have a husband
and a family but would live out your days there, perhaps being called
into the king's bedchambers at the king's whim, even after he had married someone else.

> And when Esther was taken to King Ahasuerus, into his royal palace . . . the
> king loved Esther more than all the women, and she won grace and favor
> in his sight more than all the virgins, so that he set the royal crown on her
> head and made her queen instead of Vashti. (Est. 2:16–17)

If Esther was so pleasing to the king, perhaps she was not too resistant to him. In fact, maybe she spent some time reading "How to
Please Your Man" articles in the Persian version of *Cosmopolitan* over
those twelve months of preparation. We don't know how she felt about
this—if she saw it as a great horror or a great opportunity. We do know
that this matter of the king's choosing Esther was not merely a coincidence, but that "the king's heart is a stream of water in the hand of the
Lord; he turns it wherever he will" (Prov. 21:1). God is at work here in
a way that no one can see with the human eye or understanding. "God's
plan proceeds in the world around us. It goes forward, not in spite of
our desires and inclinations, whether sinful or righteous, but precisely
through shaping us to be the people we are. . . . God's sovereignty oper-
ates in such a way that our freedom and responsibility to act are not

compromised, yet the end result is still exactly what God has purposed from the beginning. . . . God achieves his perfect goals not just through our best intentions and most self-sacrificing acts, but even through our greatest sins and compromises."[3] It may seem on the surface that King Ahasuerus has all of the power in this interplay, but really there is a hidden King in this story, and he is the one with unlimited power, which he intends to use for the good of his people, including this compromised queen.

Opposition to the Kingdom of God

In chapter 3 of Esther, we get to the heart of the story as we are introduced to Haman.

> After these things King Ahasuerus promoted Haman the Agagite, the son of Hammedatha, and advanced him and set his throne above all the officials who were with him. And all the king's servants who were at the king's gate bowed down and paid homage to Haman, for the king had so commanded concerning him. But Mordecai did not bow down or pay homage. (Est. 3:1–2)

Evidently Mordecai doesn't have a problem bowing down to the pagan king, Ahasuerus, but he refuses to bow to Haman. Why? While it isn't spelled out for us, if we had lived in the day this was written, it likely would have been clear to us when we read that Haman was an Agagite. Haman was a descendant of Agag the Amalekite. The Amalekites were the first people group to attack the children of Israel when they came out of Egypt. For this, God cursed them and condemned them to extinction (Ex. 17:8–16). Later, when Saul was crowned king, he and his armies were sent to carry out this sentence. But instead of devoting man and beast to destruction as instructed, Saul spared the best of the animals and King Agag himself. Saul left a root to regrow, which emerges here in the book of Esther as a new threat against God's people. It was because of his sparing King Agag that Saul was rejected as king. Back in Esther 2, we were told that Mordecai was "the son of Jair, son of Shimei, son of Kish" (v. 5). Remember that Saul was also called a son of Kish.

---

[3] Ibid., 69.

And when we put this together, the source of the animosity becomes clear. Modecai, a relative of King Saul, was not about to bow down to Haman, a relative of King Agag.

> And when Haman saw that Mordecai did not bow down or pay homage to him, Haman was filled with fury. But he disdained to lay hands on Mordecai alone. So, as they had made known to him the people of Mordecai, Haman sought to destroy all the Jews, the people of Mordecai, throughout the whole kingdom of Ahasuerus. (Est. 3:5–6)

Evidently just punishing Mordecai would not be enough to satisfy Haman's wounded sense of vanity. All of Mordecai's people must die. Haman wants all of the Jews living throughout the whole kingdom of Ahasuerus, which we must understand is all of the Jews living in the world, to be put

If all the Jews are killed, there will be no descendant of Abraham to bring blessing to the world, no Son of David to sit on David's throne.

to death. Really this was just the latest manifestation of Satan's ongoing warfare against the people of God, which began in the garden of Eden—the seed of the ancient Serpent seeking to destroy the seed of the woman. If all the Jews are killed, there will be no descendant of Abraham to bring blessing to the world, no Son of David to sit on David's throne. A threat to the continuation of the Jewish race was a threat to the coming of Messiah. And we begin to realize that while we might always have thought that this story is about Esther's courage to stand up for her people, really it is about God's providential care to save those from whom the Promised One will come.

Haman went to Ahasuerus, who thoughtlessly signed the decree proposed by Haman instructing people in every province to "destroy, to kill, and to annihilate all the Jews" in one day (Est. 3:13). Of course, he didn't know that his beautiful queen was a Jew. And it is at this point in the story that we discover just how isolated Esther has become from the rest of the Jewish community. Every Jew from India to Ethiopia is "fasting and weeping and lamenting" Haman's murderous edict, and Esther is oblivious to it (Est. 4:3). It would seem that Esther has not watched the news or checked her Facebook page, or maybe she just hasn't accepted friend requests from any of her old Jewish friends, because she doesn't even know that their lives are being threatened. Evidently she has done such a good job of concealing her Jewish identity that no one in the palace thought to inform her of the slaughter about to take place.

When word came to Esther that her cousin Mordecai was wearing sackcloth instead of clothes at the city gate, she sent him some clothes to put on. But he refused. Mordecai told Esther's emissary about the edict and gave him a written copy of it, "that he might show it to Esther and explain it to her and command her to go to the king to beg his favor and plead with him on behalf of her people" (Est. 4:8). God's people needed a mediator—someone who was willing and able to go where they could not go and plead their case—into the presence of the king. Initially Esther was not interested, and she sent her servant back to Mordecai with her response, saying:

> All the king's servants and the people of the king's provinces know that if any man or woman goes to the king inside the inner court without being called, there is but one law—to be put to death, except the one to whom the king holds out the golden scepter so that he may live. But as for me, I have not been called to come in to the king these thirty days. (Est. 4:11)

If Esther goes to see the king, and he does not extend to her his golden scepter, she will be put to death. It's been thirty days since she has been summoned to his bedroom to spend the night. And do we really think he's been sleeping alone with that huge house of concubines next door? It's clearly going to cost Esther something if she makes her Jewish identity known in the palace. In fact, it might cost her everything. Esther is in real danger. She is in danger of being so assimilated into the kingdom that she no longer has any identification with the people of God. She is in danger of having so capitulated to the ways of the world that she has no compassion for the people of God. And Mordecai is not backing down, sending her a response that may even contain a veiled threat.

> Do not think to yourself that in the king's palace you will escape any more than all the other Jews. For if you keep silent at this time, relief and deliverance will rise for the Jews from another place, but you and your father's house will perish. And who knows whether you have not come to the kingdom for such a time as this? (Est. 4:13–14)

We expect Mordecai to say, "If you keep silent, then your people will perish." But he doesn't. He says that if she stays silent, God will deliver the Jews in some other way. Mordecai remembers the promise made to Abraham, that through his descendants all of the nations of the earth would be blessed. He remembers God's promise to David, that one of his descendants will sit on his throne to rule forever. And he believes it. If all of the Jews in the kingdom are killed, it will be the end of God's people, the end of God's promise. And that simply can't be. Mordecai sees that Esther's being chosen as queen was not a simple twist of fate or the result of chance. He is sure that there is a greater purpose at work here. Perhaps, like Joseph, who was raised up in the palace of the Pharaoh to be in place to save his people, Esther has been raised up to the palace of Ahasuerus to save her people.

Identification with the Kingdom of God

But, of course, Esther has had no dream, as Joseph had, assuring her of future glory. She has heard no voice from heaven telling her what to do or assuring her of miraculous intervention. But she has weighed the cost and decided to act.

> Then Esther told them to reply to Mordecai, "Go, gather all the Jews to be found in Susa, and hold a fast on my behalf, and do not eat or drink for three days, night or day. I and my young women will also fast as you do. Then I will go to the king, though it is against the law, and if I perish, I perish." (Est. 4:15–16)

Esther doesn't see her death as just one possible outcome of her action but as the most likely outcome. Her statement, "If I perish, I perish," is more resignation to the inevitability of death than hope for some unexpected reprieve. She put on her best dress and stood outside the king's throne room, and when he saw her, he invited her in. Instead of cutting to the chase and pleading for the lives of her people, Esther invited the king and Haman to a private banquet. The next night at the banquet, once again she didn't broach the topic of the edict to kill the Jews but invited the king and Haman to come back the next night.

But the night in between the two banquets, the king couldn't sleep. In an attempt to lull himself to sleep, the king asked for what may have been the most boring reading material available—a history book. Or maybe he was looking for what would be the most interesting reading material to a self-obsessed king—a book all about himself and his accomplishments. Whichever it was, God was at work through ordinary insomnia and choice of reading material as the king discovered in his reading that he had never publicly rewarded someone who had notified him of a plot against his life—Mordecai. If you want people to be willing to come forward and inform you about possible threats on your life, it's a good idea to handsomely reward those who do.

On the same night, Haman could hardly sleep either. On his way home, feeling so good about himself as the only person included in the royal banquet, he walked by that Jew, Mordecai, who refused to bow. So he went to bed making mental plans for the gallows he would build to hang Mordecai. The next day when Haman got to the king's court, the king was waiting to ask him a question: "What should be done to the man whom the king delights to honor?" (Est. 6:6). And, of course, Haman was quite sure that he must be the man the king wanted to honor. So he thought through exactly how he would like to be honored and laid it out for the king.

> For the man whom the king delights to honor, let royal robes be brought, which the king has worn, and the horse that the king has ridden, and on whose head a royal crown is set. And let the robes and the horse be handed over to one of the king's most noble officials. Let them dress the man whom the king delights to honor, and let them lead him on the horse through the square of the city, proclaiming before him: "Thus shall it be done to the man whom the king delights to honor." (Est. 6:7–9)

But, of course, the king had in mind honoring Mordecai, the very person Haman has hoped to hang on the gallows he was having built.

The feast of pleasurable thoughts he enjoyed the night before about the hanging of Mordecai went sour in his stomach. Imagine the frustration and humiliation he must have felt as he walked through the streets of Susa giving Mordecai the elaborate honor that he had hoped would be heaped upon him. At least he had another banquet with the queen that night to look forward to.

The queen, meanwhile, had kept a secret ever since she was taken into the royal harem—her belonging to the people of God. But it was time to make her true identity known. That night at the second banquet with the king and Haman she said:

> If I have found favor in your sight, O king, and if it please the king, let my life be granted me for my wish, and my people for my request. For we have been sold, I and my people, to be destroyed, to be killed, and to be annihilated. (Est. 7:3–4)

Esther has now effectively added her name to the list of those to be slaughtered on the appointed day. She has left behind compromise and hiding to identify herself with God's people and their plight.

> Then King Ahasuerus said to Queen Esther, "Who is he, and where is he, who has dared to do this?" And Esther said, "A foe and enemy! This wicked Haman!" (Est. 7:5–6)

We can almost see and hear the drama in silent, black-and-white film. And so Haman was hanged on the gallows he had prepared for Mordecai. And it would seem that the story is over, as Esther has not perished and the evil Haman is dead. The seed of the woman, Esther, has risen to crush the head of the seed of the Serpent, Haman. But there remains that pesky detail of an edict that has gone out throughout all of the provinces, setting a day for all of the Jews to be slaughtered—an edict that cannot be revoked.

> Then Esther spoke again to the king. . . . She said, "If it please the king, and if I have found favor in his sight, and if the thing seems right before the king, and I am pleasing in his eyes, let an order be written to revoke the letters devised by Haman the Agagite, the son of Hammedatha, which he

> wrote to destroy the Jews who are in all the provinces of the king. For how
> can I bear to see the calamity that is coming to my people? Or how can I
> bear to see the destruction of my kindred?" (Est. 8:3–6)

Esther has come all of the way out of the closet. She is no longer cunningly coy. She is at the king's feet weeping and pleading for the lives of the people of God. And the king responds by telling her that she and Mordecai can issue a counteracting edict however they see fit. So they sent out a decree saying that the Jews in every province could defend their lives and kill anyone who attacked them. And that is exactly what happened.

> On the very day when the enemies of the Jews hoped to gain the mastery
> over them, the reverse occurred: the Jews gained mastery over those who
> hated them. (Est. 9:1)

The kingdom of Ahasuerus provides us with a stark contrast to the kingdom of God under King Jesus.

Those who set themselves against the people of God, hoping to dominate and destroy them, were themselves destroyed. And so ends a great story of deliverance of the people of God. But, really, it is just one chapter in a much larger story, an ongoing battle between the kingdom of darkness and the kingdom of God.

Salvation in the Kingdom of God

If you remember, we started our study of the historical books of the Old Testament talking about the kingdom of God and what it is like when his kingdom comes. And the book of Esther actually helps to fill out that picture more completely, as the kingdom of Ahasuerus provides us with a stark contrast to the kingdom of God under King Jesus.

When the kingdom of God comes in our lives, we come under a wise King, one who does not need the input of his underlords to know what to do. Even now our King is working in hidden, invisible ways, bringing about his sovereign plans for history, but one day the whole world will see him and bow before him.

The feast we are served in his kingdom is more grand than that of King Ahasuerus's. It is the bread of his broken body and the cup of the covenant in his blood, which nourishes our very souls. But, really, our Communion meal is just an appetizer, whetting our appetite for the great banquet to come, the wedding supper of the lamb, which we will enjoy in the presence of our King.

Our King is not a self-absorbed bachelor who would banish his bride from his kingdom on a drunken whim. He does not ignore his bride and is not unfaithful to his bride. Our bridegroom loves his bride purely and permanently. Even now he is making us beautiful, not through pampering but through pruning, not through soaking in baths of oil and spices but by soaking in the Word of God, not by living secluded in luxury but by entering into the suffering of the world around us. Our King was marred and made as one from whom men hide their faces in order that we might become his beautiful bride.

In this greater kingdom we have a better mediator than Esther. Our mediator was well aware of our need and unconcerned with preserving his own life. He did not have to be cajoled to take up our cause but covenanted with the Father and the Spirit in eternity past to intercede for us—not at the risk of his life but at the cost of his life. He was willing to perish so that we will "not perish but have eternal life" (John 3:16).

Because the fierce rod of judgment fell upon Christ, God can extend the golden scepter of his favor toward us. We need have no fear to approach the throne. We can come knowing that we will be welcomed and not condemned, confident that we will "receive mercy and find grace to help in time of need." (Heb. 4:16)

We were born into a kingdom under an irrevocable decree that threatens our very lives, which is this: "For the wages of sin is death." But our King has issued another decree that will be our salvation, which is: "but the free gift of God is eternal life in Christ Jesus our Lord" (Rom. 6:23).

The pull of the pleasures of the kingdom of this world is strong. This kingdom wants to assimilate us so that we look like everyone else and think like everyone else and value what everyone else values. But the kingdom of God calls us away from that. It calls us to identify ourselves with the people of God. It may mean being hated and marginalized in this world, but it holds out great reward, a great reversal of fortunes, when his kingdom comes. Jesus told his disciples:

> They will lay their hands on you and persecute you, delivering you up to the synagogues and prisons, and you will be brought before kings and governors for my name's sake. This will be your opportunity to bear witness. Settle it therefore in your minds not to meditate beforehand how to answer, for I will give you a mouth and wisdom, which none of your adversaries will be able to withstand or contradict. You will be delivered up even by parents and brothers and relatives and friends, and some of you they will put to death. You will be hated by all for my name's sake. But not a hair of your head will perish. By your endurance you will gain your lives. (Luke 21:12–19)

You see, even if you are put to death because of your identification with the people of God and your allegiance to your great King, you will not ultimately perish. Instead you can be sure that by losing your life in the service of your King, you will have preserved it.

Looking Forward
You Will Surely Fall before Him
On the night of the first banquet given by Queen Esther, Haman left the banquet elated. But he was furious by the time he got home, because he had passed by Mordecai who would not bow to him. Feeding and affirming his rage, his wife and friends told him just what he should do: "Let a gallows fifty cubits high be made, and in the morning tell the king to have Mordecai hanged upon it" (Est. 5:14). Haman liked the idea and initiated building the gallows the next morning.

But things didn't go at all as expected that day. In a stunning reversal of fortunes, Haman spent the day honoring Mordecai instead of hanging him. That night when he got home and told his wife and friends what had happened, they made a 180-degree turn from their message to Haman the night before.

His wise men and his wife Zeresh said to him, "If Mordecai, before whom you have begun to fall, is of the Jewish people, you
will not overcome him but will surely fall before him." (Est. 6:13)

Why would they say this? Why are they sure that since Mordecai is
Jewish, Haman will be unable to defeat him? Throughout Israel's history God repeatedly intervened on their behalf to bring defeat on their
enemies and deliverance for his people. So perhaps they had heard all
about that history. Evidently those surrounding Haman recognized
that the stunning turn of events that day was not just mere coincidence but was the sovereign hand of God at work doing what he has
always promised to do—preserve a people for himself. Perhaps they
were familiar with the words of the prophet Isaiah, who had said to
God's people about two hundred years earlier: "Whoever stirs up strife
with you shall fall because of you. . . . No weapon that is fashioned
against you shall succeed" (Isa. 54:15, 17). Haman has set himself
against God by setting himself against God's people, and even though
his wife and wise men are pagans who do not bow the knee to Israel's
God, they know enough about Israel's history to know that if God is
for the Jews, who can stand against them?

This was good news not only for the people of God in Esther's day
but also for the people of God in our day—especially those who live in
parts of the world in which believers are under constant threat of violence. All the powers of evil are under God's control, and he will defend
his people. He alone accomplishes the promised victory. He will protect
his people and defeat every enemy, no matter how powerful. Indeed it
is impossible for God's people to ultimately perish. As Jesus said, "Do
not fear those who kill the body but cannot kill the soul. Rather fear him
who can destroy both soul and body in hell" (Matt. 10:28).

In the end, there will once again be a stunning reversal of fortunes. All of those who have set themselves against God by setting
themselves against God's people will bow before the true King. There
will be a great righting of wrongs. Point by point, evil will be over-
turned and replaced with right by the authority of the King. Though
many powers are at work in the world for evil, the true King of kings
will defeat them all.

Discussion Guide

Esther ~~Esther~~

ester   *esther*

Getting the Discussion Going

1. The writer of the book of Esther seems content to be ambiguous about Esther's faith and piety and morality. What are your impressions about why Esther does what she does?

Obedient to Mordecai

Getting to the Heart of It

2. Esther is a book of the Bible in which God is not even mentioned. But certainly he is assumed and active. How do you see God at work in this story? *directing hearts*

3. The book of Esther encourages us to contrast the kingdom of the world under King Ahasuerus with the kingdom of God under King Jesus. Think through some of the actions and attitudes of King Ahasuerus. In what ways is it far better to live in the kingdom of God under King Jesus? *we can approach Him*

4. The goal of the kingdom of Persia in Esther's day was assimilation. Do you think the kingdom of the world in our day demands assimilation? In what ways do you see it? *communication*

5. Romans 12:2 instructs, "Do not be conformed to this world, but be transformed by the renewal of your mind, that by testing you may dis-

cern what is the will of God, what is good and acceptable and perfect."
What do you think that means, and what do you think it requires?

be so enveloped in the word

6. Someone read aloud John 15:18–25 and John 16:32–33. How is
this truth demonstrated in history, especially in the book of Esther, and
what does it tell us about what we can expect in the future?

If the world hates Jesus they will hate us

7. Haman is one in a long line of enemies of the people of God who are
really shills of the ancient Serpent. Who are some of the other char-
acters or powers throughout Old Testament history that fall into this
category? And how was each of them defeated?

Daniel (king advisors)

Getting Personal

thank you

8. Can you relate to Nancy's fear and reluctance to go public with identifying herself with Christ as the only way of knowing God? Have you
experienced opposition directly related to your stand for Christ? If not,
why do you think that is?

work

Getting How It Fits into the Big Picture

9. When Jesus walked with the two disciples on the road to Emmaus,
and "beginning with Moses and all the Prophets, he interpreted to them
in all the Scriptures the things concerning himself" (Luke 24:27), what
do you think he might have said about how the book of Esther was
about him?

Bibliography

Books and Articles

Blackham, Paul. *Joshua Book by Book Study Guide*. London: Biblical Frameworks, 2010.

Chapman, Colin. *Whose Promised Land: Israel or Palestine*. Oxford, UK: Lion, 1992.

Davis, Dale Ralph. *Such a Great Salvation: Expositions of the Book of Judges*. Grand Rapids, MI: Baker, 1990.

Dever, Mark. *The Message of the Old Testament: Promises Made*. Wheaton, IL: Crossway, 2006.

DeYoung, Kevin. "Thinking about the Kingdom." http://thegospelcoalition.org/blogs/kevindeyoung/2009/10/07/thinking-about-kingdom/.

Duguid, Iain M. *Esther and Ruth*. Reformed Expository Commentary. Phillipsburg, NJ: P&R, 2005.

Gibson, David. "Bible Overview 3: The Promised Kingdom and Partial Kingdom Part 2" "Beginning with Moses? http://beginningwithmoses.org/bt-articles/198/bible-overview-3-the-promised-kingdom-partial-kingdom-part-2-.

Goldsworthy, Graeme. *The Goldsworthy Trilogy*. Exeter, UK: Paternoster, 2000.

Guthrie, Nancy. *The One Year Book of Discovering Jesus in the Old Testament*. Carol Stream, IL: Tyndale, 2010.

Jobes, Karen. *Esther*. The NIV Application Commentary. Grand Rapids, MI: Zondervan, 1999.

Ladd, George Eldon. *The Gospel of the Kingdom*. Grand Rapids, MI: Eerdmans, 1959.

Leithart, Peter. *1 and 2 Kings*. Brazos Theological Commentary on the Bible. Grand Rapids, MI: Brazos Press, 2006.

Martens, Elmer A. *God's Design: A Focus on Old Testament Theology*. North Richland Hills, TX: D. & F. Scott, 1998.

Provan, Iain William, V. Philips Long, and Tremper Longman. *A Biblical History of Israel*. Louisville: Westminster, 2003.

Riddlebarger, Kim. "The Drama of Redemption: Joshua." Sermon series. Christ Reformed Church. Anaheim, CA, 2007. http://www.christreformed.org/kim-riddlebarger/#Joshua.

Robertson, O. Palmer. *The Israel of God: Yesterday, Today, and Tomorrow*. Phillipsburg, NJ: P&R, 2000.

Ryken, Philip Graham. *King Solomon: The Temptations of Money, Sex, and Power*. Wheaton, IL: Crossway, 2011.

Schwab, George M. *Right in Their Own Eyes: The Gospel According to Judges.* Phillipsburg, NJ: P&R, 2011.

Smith, Colin S. *Unlocking the Bible Story.* Chicago: Moody, 2002.

Ulrich, Dean R. *From Famine to Fullness: The Gospel according to Ruth.* Phillipsburg, NJ: P&R, 2007.

Um, Stephen. *The Kingdom of God.* Gospel Coalition Booklet. Wheaton, IL: Crossway, 2011.

Williams, Michael D. *Far as the Curse Is Found: The Covenant Story of Redemption.* Phillipsburg, NJ: P&R, 2005.

Woodhouse, John. *1 Samuel: Looking for a Leader.* Preaching the Word. Wheaton, IL: Crossway, 2008.

Audio

Ash, Christopher. "Esther." Sermon series. All Saints Little Shelford, UK, 2000.

Begg, Alistair. "Seeing What David Saw." Sermon. Parkside Church. Chagrin Falls, Ohio, October 24, 2004.

Blackham, Paul. "Enter the Queen of Sheba." Sermon. All Souls Langham Place. London, February 16, 2003.

———. "How to Win a Battle." Sermon. All Souls Langham Place. London, February 15, 2004.

Blackham, Paul, Rico Tice, and Richard Bewes. "Building the Church." Sermon series on Nehemiah. All Souls Langham Place. London. 2001.

Blackham, Paul, and Christopher Wright. "Entering into the Promises." Sermon series on Joshua. All Souls Langham Place. London, 2004.

Campbell "Who Am I?" Sermon. Point Free Church. Isle of Lewis, Scotland, October 4, 2009.

Coekin, Richard. "The Inheritance We Await." Sermon. Saint Andrews @ Seven, Wimbledon, UK, October, 19, 2008.

Cosper, Mike. "Esther." Sermon. Union University. Jackson, TN, March 4, 2011.

Dennis, Jon. "The Hiddenness of God in a Life That Matters." Sermon series on Esther. Holy Trinity Church. Chicago. 2011.

DeYoung, Kevin. "Ezra." Sermon Series. University Reformed Church. Lansing, MI, 2012.

Goligher, Liam. "The Covenant-Making God." Sermon. Tenth Presbyterian Church. Philadelphia, PA, May 13, 2012.

———. "Giant Killer." Sermon. Duke Street Church. London, November 13, 2011.

———."The Romance of Redemption." Sermon series on Ruth. Duke Street Church, London, 2007.

Helm, David. "Nehemiah." Sermon series. Holy Trinity Church. Chicago, 2006.

———. "Ruth." Sermon series. Holy Trinity Church. Chicago, 2003.

Jackman, David. "Voice of the Prophets: Solomon to Exile" The Christian Institute. Newcastle, UK, September 16, 1994.

Keller, Timothy J. "An Immigrant's Courage." Sermon. Redeemer Presbyterian Church. New York, October 19, 1997.

———. "Joshua and the General." Sermon. Redeemer Presbyterian Church. New York, September 22, 1996.

———. "The Promise of David." Sermon. Redeemer Presbyterian Church. New York, December 14, 2003.

Larroux, Jean. "The Crown" Sermon. Southwood Presbyterian Church. Huntsville, AL, April 8, 2012.

———. "Your Will Be Done on Earth as It Is in Heaven." Sermon. Lagniappe Church. Bay St. Louis, MS, June 22, 2008.

Lucas, Sean Michael. "God Only Wise" Sermon. Covenant Presbyterian Church. St. Louis, MO, July 24, 2005.

Moody, Josh. "If You Want God, You Have to Get Over Your Self." Sermon series on Judges. College Church. Wheaton, IL, 2009.

Olyott, Stuart. "Promised Land to Exile" Sermon series. Belvidere Road Church. Liverpool, UK, 1979.

Ortlund, Raymond C. "The Outpouring of the Holy Spirit." Sermon. Christ Presbyterian Church. Nashville, TN. February 26, 2006.

———. "What the Bible Is All About, 11." Sermon. Christ Presbyterian Church. Nashville, TN. May 29, 2005.

Piper, John. "God's Covenant with David." Sermon. Bethlehem Baptist Church. Minneapolis, MN, December 18, 1983.

———. "The Importance of the Kingdom Today." Sermon. Bethlehem Baptist Church. Minneapolis, MN, January 28, 1990.

———. "Is the Kingdom Present or Future?" Sermon. Bethlehem Baptist Church. Minneapolis, MN. February 4, 1990.

Woodhouse, John. "God's People: Who Are They? What Are They Like? What Do They Do?" Sermon series on Ezra and Nehemiah. Christ Church. St. Ives, Australia. 1993.

———. "The History of Israel: Joshua to 2 Kings." Sermon. Christ Church. St. Ives, Australia.

Wookey, Stephen. "The Endless Cycle." All Souls Langham Place. London, February 26, 1995.

Wright, Christopher. "A Bold Proposal." Sermon. All Souls Langham Place. London, May 27, 2007.

For additional content, downloads,
and resources for leaders, please visit:

www.SeeingJesusInTheOldTestament.com

Also Available in the
Seeing Jesus in the Old Testament Series

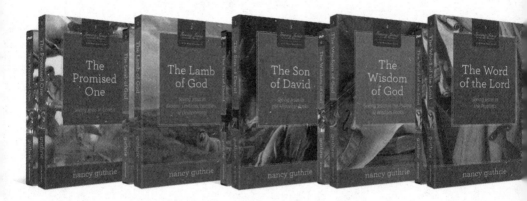

The Promised One: *Seeing Jesus in Genesis*

The Lamb of God: *Seeing Jesus in Exodus, Leviticus, Numbers, and Deuteronomy*

The Son of David: *Seeing Jesus in the Historical Books*

The Wisdom of God: *Seeing Jesus in the Psalms and Wisdom Books*

The Word of the Lord: *Seeing Jesus in the Prophets*

A companion DVD is also available for each study.